CHRIST

in the Old Testament

CHRIST
in the Old Testament

by

T. W. CALLAWAY, D.D.

LOIZEAUX BROTHERS

New York

FIRST EDITION, SEPTEMBER 1950
SECOND PRINTING, JUNE 1958

PRINTED IN THE UNITED STATES OF AMERICA

ACKNOWLEDGMENT

Much of the information contained in this book has been accumulated by the author over a period of years from books read, sermons, Bible conferences, and many other sources, the authors of which are unknown. To all who have in any way contributed to its production we are profoundly grateful and make acknowledgments. The author claims but little originality for the views and interpretations contained in this book.

Our aim is to make *Christ in the Old Testament* informative, simple, and easy to understand, doctrinally scriptural, interesting, and to glorify Christ.

To Rev. R. Lofton Hudson, M.A., Ph.D., now pastor of the First Baptist Church, Shawnee, Oklahoma, who first read the manuscript and made many helpful suggestions, the author is sincerely grateful.

T. W. CALLAWAY

James Island
Charleston, South Carolina
April 1950

To the students
of the Mountain Preachers Bible School,
Clear Creek Springs, Pineville, Kentucky,
true comrades of the author,
whose labor as a member of the faculty was one of love,
this volume is affectionately dedicated.

CONTENTS

INTRODUCTION

THE ORIGIN AND SUBSTANCE OF CHRIS-
tianity is the Person, Jehovah-Christ. His history is the
outgrowth of the Jewish life and doctrine of the Old Testament. Working upon the assurance that the truthfulness of
these Old Testament Scriptures is of the highest evidential
value, it becomes a helpful and fascinating study to find
Christ in the Old Testament: "Jesus Christ, the same yester-
day, today, and forever." [1] This book is to emphasize the
importance of understanding the Bible with its typical and
prophetic messages.

Jehovah-Christ, the eternal One, is the theme of the entire Scriptures, the center of all Christian doctrine. The
Bible was written with that in view, and any other viewpoint produces a dwarfed conception of Christ. "What think
ye of the Christ?" is just as applicable to the Old Covenant
as to the New. The gospel should not be limited to the New
Testament, as an intelligent apprehension of Christ is as
truly manifested in the Old. Most of Paul's arguments were
based on Old Testament Scriptures, as we may see in the
tenth chapter of Romans. He explained that the gospel he
preached was according to the Old Testament Scriptures.[2]
He reminded Timothy that "From a child thou hast known
the holy [O.T.] Scriptures." To the Galatians Paul wrote:
"And the Scripture [O.T.] . . . preached before the gospel
unto Abraham." Peter and other apostles proved their messages from the Old Testament. Therefore, it proves a defec-

1. Heb. 13:8; Rom. 15:4; 1 Cor. 10:11
2. 1 Cor. 15:1-4; 2 Tim. 3:15; 2 Pet. 1:20,21

tive conception of the eternal Christ not to see Him in the entire Scriptures.

The aim of this book is to discover the historical source of the name, JEHOVAH-CHRIST, and to trace it through the centuries, in type, symbol, prophecy, and figure of speech, finding its connection between the apocalyptic Messiah of the Old Testament, and the Saviour of the New.

Not all language of the Old Testament is to be interpreted literally. The Bible contains many figures of speech. However, this does not warrant the type of interpretation called "spiritualization" which renders language meaningless and without foundation. A type is a "divinely planned unfolding of future events, pertaining to a person, place, event, object, or institution." A thing is not to be taken as a type unless the New Testament directly states that it is, or unless there is very clear evidence in the analogy that such typology really exists. Jesus based His gospel upon the foundation laid in the Old Testament. The symbolism of the Old Testament is lost unless one sees in it the basis of the New. The purpose of God in the Old Testament finds its consummation in the gospel of the Messiah. His coming was heralded in the promises of the ancient prophets, in the words of the angel to Mary and Elisabeth, as well as through the Magnificat and the Benedicite. The greatness of Christ is evidenced in His dealings with the Old Testament revelation.

Someone has said that the "Old Testament is the *foreshadowing* of the New, and that the New Testament is the *unfolding* of the Old: the Old anticipates, promises, and foreshadows the New, while the New authenticates, performs, and fulfills the Old." Augustine is credited with saying that the "New Testament is *concealed* in the Old, and the Old is *revealed* in the New: that the New is in the Old *contained*, while the Old is in the New *explained*." Another has said that "we cannot know Christ apart from the Bible, nor the Bible apart from Christ."

"Other foundation can no man lay than that which is laid, which is Jesus Christ." [3] Christ believed the Old Testament Scriptures as referring to Himself, saying:

> O fools, and slow of heart to believe all that the prophets have spoken . . . And beginning at Moses and all the prophets, He expounded unto them in all the Scriptures the things concerning Himself . . . which were written in the law of Moses, and in the prophets, and in the psalms, concerning Me. [4]

Christ and His gospel are easily found in the Old Testament and were proclaimed by Jehovah to His people in olden times. Men were to worship Him, the Righteous, the Holy One, and not idols. Noah preached the gospel of the righteousness of God and the judgment to come. Enoch, the seventh from Adam, proclaimed the gospel of Christ's second advent. Daniel told when "transgressors are come to the full," and Abraham was given the glad tidings of his "Seed" blessing the earth. [5]

3. 1 Cor. 3:11
4. Luke 24:25,27,44
5. Heb. 11:7; 2 Pet. 2:5; Dan. 8:23; Gen. 12:1-3; 15:4; Gal. 3:16

The Scripture references in the footnotes are not confined to quotations within the chapter, but present a general view of the subjects covered.

Chapter 1

"JEHOVAH"
of the Old Testament
the Christ of the New

CHRISTIANITY AND MORALITY FIND their foundation in a personal God. Final authority is vested in Him. JEHOVAH-CHRIST is God's revelation in life and service.

There are some 830 quotations in the New Testament from the Old, many pointing to Christ, some 250 written from 1500 to 400 B.C., of which every prophetic detail has been minutely fulfilled; 208 times in the Bible it is claimed that God is its Author; 6855 times the name of the LORD (JEHOVAH) appears.

We are to study the Person of Christ as revealed in His names, finding their fulfilment in their power and beauty. "In Him dwelleth all the fulness of the Godhead bodily." A name in the Old Testament is often indicative of a person's character. Here the compound names of Jehovah reveal His work and character in relation to His creatures.

The first name of God in the Bible is the Hebrew ELOHIM, a uniplural noun, suggesting the Trinity, and also emphasizing the plurality of His majesty and power.[1] The same thought is expressed in Deuteronomy 6:4, "Hear, O Israel: the Lord our God is *one* Lord." The word "one" in the Hebrew here means "many in one," as Adam and Eve were

1. Gen. 1:1,3,26; 35:7; Deut. 6:4

said to be "one flesh." God said, "Let *us* make man in *our* image." [2] The word ELOHIM (God) appears 2570 times in the Bible, and 32 times in the first chapter of Genesis. ELOHIM means "mighty," "strong One," "omnipotent," "sovereign," "the great originator," bringing order out of chaos. The term, "In the beginning," is the same as it is in the first chapter of John, and is so translated in the Greek Septuagint. It has reference to eternity; Christ co-eternal with the Father before creation.

The second name of God in the Old Testament is EL-SHADDAI and is translated "Almighty God." It appears 48 times in the Old Testament. This name God gave Himself to Abraham. It means "God All-sufficient"—all-bountiful; the God of power to nourish, supply, satisfy—the God that is enough, and to chasten His people. He is the covenant-keeping God in whom we are blessed with power, wisdom, redemption, and preservation, the strong One in grace.[3]

In the names of God we find development. First as ELOHIM in the plural form, then as mighty EL-SHADDAI, and then as the JEHOVAH, who is to appear in human form as Redeemer and to live among men. JEHOVAH is to be connected with all creation, both animate and inanimate, displaying His marvelous grace for the redemption of mankind. JEHOVAH-CHRIST is now to have a new companionship —a redeemed company of believers—as His personal possession:[4]

> Who hath saved us, and called us with an holy calling, not according to our works, but according to His own purpose and grace, which was given us in Christ Jesus before the world began.

2. Gen. 1:26; 2:24; John 1:1
3. Gen. 17:1-8
4. Gen. 2:4,5; 4:1; 12:1; Ex. 3:14; John 1:41; 4:25; 2 Tim. 1:9; **Ex.** 3:14

This third name of God, Jehovah, translated Lord in the English language, first appears in Genesis 2:4. This name is the summary of the Person, work, history, glory, and nature of Christ. The Old Testament has some 200 titles for Christ, revealing the fulness of His nature, and the many-sided relationship to His people. However, Jehovah is the self-revealing One in family relationship to His people. It is a proper noun and never plural as Elohim, being derived from the Hebrew verb *Havah,* to be, or being. Jehovah is the Christ-Messiah, the Anointed One, first mentioned in creation, then as Redeemer, and is the new and definite name of God.

The meaning of the word Jehovah is the Supreme One, the Living One, unchangeable, self-existent in the work of creation; to live, to breathe, eternal, Divine Being; the immutable One, source of Life—who was, is, and is the coming One—the ever present One, the Christ of providence, the Covenant-keeper in relation to His own. He is

> The great I Am—the everlasting God-Jehovah,
> the Creator of the ends of the earth . . . I, Jehovah,
> the first and the last . . . besides Me there is no
>   God . . .
> from the time that it was, there am I.

Jehovah says:

> I Am the God of Abraham—Type of the Father of a
>   nation.[5]
> I Am the God of Isaac—Type of the Son of promise.
> I Am the God of Jacob—Type of the Spirit, "sup-
>   planter."

When God would make a special revelation of Himself, He used the name Jehovah, expressing His moral and spiritual attributes in love, holiness, and righteousness. The message of Jehovah-Christ to Israel by Moses was:

5. Isa. 43:10,11; Ex. 3:6,7

And I appeared unto Abraham, unto Isaac, and unto Jacob, by the name of God Almighty, but by my name JEHOVAH was I not known to them.[6]

JEHOVAH is showing Israel that He is their Deliverer, thus winning their gratitude.

The Person and work of JEHOVAH (Hebrew, *Yah-Yahweh;* Greek, *Iesus;* English, *Jesus*) is seen in the compound names used in the Old Testament. These are mentioned as "Jehovah Titles," portraying His character in meeting human needs. The first of these compound names is JEHOVAH-JIREH, meaning "Jehovah, our Provider," or "Jehovah will provide." It is found in the great crisis in the life of Abraham and Isaac, commemorating a great deliverance. Here is a double-type. God is showing that Christ is the Lamb provided in the deliverance of Isaac through the provision of a substitute. The "ram," as a substitute, typified Christ on the Cross. Christ became the "scapegoat" for the sinner. JEHOVAH-CHRIST is showing His wonderful grace and provision, providence, and purpose. It also displays the faith and obedience of Abraham.

"Seeing thou hast not withheld thy son, thine only son from Me." Isaac is a type of one under judgment, the lamb becoming his substitute. John the Baptist cried:

Behold the Lamb of God, which taketh away the sin of the world.[7]

The second compound title is JEHOVAH-ROPHEKA, meaning "Jehovah that healeth thee." Here Christ the Healer is showing that every harmful thing in the life of the believer can come under the healing and restoring power of the Great Physician. This name appears first in Exodus 15:22-26. It comes from the experiences of Israel in crossing the Red Sea and singing the song of triumph.

6. Psa. 11:7; Lev. 19:23; Ex. 6:3
7. Gen. 22:8,13,14; Psa. 23:5; Phil. 4:19; Heb. 11:18,19; John 1:29

JEHOVAH-ROPHEKA is also the Great Physician in a moral and spiritual sense. He is the Christ-healer of the New Testament. The physical healings of Christ were incidental. They were the credentials of His mission. The healing of the souls of men was His great objective. He became the "Water of Life," the "Well of Salvation." [8]

The third compound title of JEHOVAH is JEHOVAH-NISSI, meaning "Jehovah my Banner," showing Christ as Victor, the Captain under whose banner the Christian conquers. Israel had come to Rephidim where there was no water. They encountered their enemy, the Amalekites, descendants of Esau, a powerful and implacable foe. Israel was finally victorious. Moses held the God-given rod that led Israel through the Red Sea.

> Moses built an altar, and called the name of it Jehovah-Nissi, Jehovah is my Banner.

As a banner of JEHOVAH this rod was an emblem of victory, an earnest of His power and presence. In the power of "Jehovah my Banner" Israel waged her warfare. It is so with the believer today who will put on the "whole armour of God." In His strength come victory and triumph.[9]

The fourth compound title of JEHOVAH is JEHOVAH-M'KADDISHKEM, and is the "I AM Jehovah that sanctify you"; Christ, the Sanctifier. This name is repeated seven times in three chapters of Leviticus, showing the purpose of God as relating to the needs of His people. The book of Leviticus instructs the redeemed how to live and walk. Sanctification is the theme:

> I AM the coming One who sanctifieth thee.

8. Ex. 15:26; Job 5:18; Isa. 61:1; 12:3; 30:26; Psa. 103:2,3; Luke 4:18
9. 2 Chron. 13:12-16; Eph. 6:10-12; 2 Cor. 2:14

The priests were set apart, clean, separated, undefiled, without spot or blemish in approaching God. "Holiness to Jehovah" was upon the crown of the High Priest.

> Follow peace with all men, and holiness, without which no man shall see the Lord.

Holiness is an attribute of God. He demands and imparts "righteousness and true holiness" to those that would approach Him in the Most Holy Place. The sanctification of Jehovah means not only relation, but also participation, in process as well as position, objective as well as subjective, right positionally and conditionally.

This is a glorious name for those that crave God's best for their lives, not only judicially but in experience. It is the indwelling, empowering, Jehovah-Sanctifier that enables His holy ones to live a holy life.[10]

The fifth compound title is JEHOVAH-SHALOM, meaning "Jehovah My Peace" or prosperity. Gideon built an altar and called it JEHOVAH-SHALOM. Israel had been corrupt in idolatry and void of purity, prayer, and prosperity.

> There is no peace, saith the Lord, to the wicked.

Israel was living a materialistic life and was in slavery. God was child-training His own who were subdued by the Midianites. The angel of the Lord appeared to Gideon with a promise of deliverance. Hence the altar, "Jehovah is Peace." Gideon was expressing a heart need. This name is used also in connection with the Peace Offering. It is the source of all lasting peace.

> Thou wilt keep him in perfect peace, whose mind is stayed on Thee.

10. Ex. 31:13; Lev. 19:2-37; 20:8; 22:32; Heb. 3:1; 12:14; 2 Tim. 1:9; 1 Cor. 1:30; Eph. 4:24; Ex. 28:36

Gideon did not erect an altar of sacrifice from the *penalty* of sin, but of *peace* in service, free from the power and dominion of sin. JEHOVAH-CHRIST is peace, making reconciliation:

Having made peace through the blood of His cross.

It is not only the privilege of the believer to have "peace *with* God," but also to have the "peace *of* God" that passeth all understanding.

Peace given, procured at the cross—Salvation.
Peace filling, secured in Christ—Dedication.
Peace abiding, assured by the Word—Participation.

Christ *became* peace—"He is our peace."
Christ *made* peace—"So making peace."
Christ *proclaimed* peace—"And preached peace." [11]

Another compound title of Jehovah is JEHOVAH-ZIDKENU, meaning "Jehovah our Righteousness."

And this is His name whereby He shall be called: Jehovah our Righteousness.

Judah had sinned against God and was about to fall. Priests and people were guilty.

And Jehovah said, I will remove Judah also out of my sight, as I have removed Israel.

God would have Judah confess her guilt and acknowledge His righteousness. The meaning of JEHOVAH-ZIDKENU carries with it the idea of justification, or being made righteous, which brings about a just and righteous relationship. Christ provides present judicial and objective righteousness in salvation, subjective and personal righteousness for service, and future progressive and character righteousness in development. This will never be completed until the saints

11. Judges 6:24; Isa. 9:6; Lev. 3; Lev. 7; Isa. 26:3; Rom. 5:1; 15:13; Phil. 4:7; Eph. 2:14,15,17; Col. 1:20

see Him face to face. JEHOVAH-ZIDKENU provides and becomes the righteousness of the believer. In Him are found justice and righteousness. "In Jehovah . . . have I righteousness." As the Source of righteousness He could say:

> The sins of Judah . . . they shall not be found: for I will pardon them.

Here God's amazing grace is shown.

> Abraham believed God and it was reckoned to him for righteousness.

This imputed righteousness of the JEHOVAH-CHRIST makes the sinner acceptable to God. Christ is the righteous One. The believer receives His righteousness as a free gift through faith in Him.[12]

Another compound title is JEHOVAH-SHAMMAH, meaning "The Lord is there." This name has to do with the transformation of everything and all of God's children. Where there is no JEHOVAH-SHAMMAH everything is ruin, defeat, darkness, tears, and death. Israel today is without her JEHOVAH-SHAMMAH. The Lord is not in their midst. However, the Shekinah glory of JEHOVAH-SHAMMAH shall return to Israel if perchance there might be a heartfelt repentance. She can look ahead to the time when JEHOVAH-SHAMMAH shall return with the realization of eternal blessing, when all wrongs will have been righted and all evils forgotten, because of JEHOVAH-SHAMMAH, "the Lord is there."

There are ten of these compound "Jehovah titles." Among those not previously mentioned are: JEHOVAH-ZEBAOTH, meaning "Jehovah of Hosts"; and JEHOVAH-ELYON, meaning "Jehovah Most High," seen as Prophet, Priest, and King.

The most beloved compound name is that of JEHOVAH-Ro'I, meaning "Jehovah my Shepherd." It will be noticed

12. Jer. 23:5,6; 33:16; 2 Kings 23:27; Job 25:4; Isa. 45:24; Gen. 15:6; 1 Cor. 1:2,30; 1 John 3:2; 2 Cor. 5:21; Phil. 3:9

that seven of these "Jehovah titles" are referred to in the twenty-third Psalm, showing His attributes in behalf of His sheep; namely,[13]

JEHOVAH-JIREH—"I shall not want"—provider—verse 1
JEHOVAH-SHALOM—"Beside the still waters"—Peace—
    verse 2
JEHOVAH-ROPHEKA ⎱ —"He restoreth my soul"—
JEHOVAH-TSIDKENU ⎰ Healer—verse 3
JEHOVAH-M'KADDISHKEM ⎱—"Thou anointest my head"
JEHOVAH-NISSI   ⎰—Sanctifier—verse 5
JEHOVAH-SHAMMAH—"Thou art with me"—Guide—
    verse 4

Thank God for the Good, Great, and Chief Shepherd, JEHOVAH-RO'I.

13. 1 Sam. 1:3; Ez. 48:35; Isa. 46:9,10; Psa. 7:17; 47:2; Deut. 18:18; Jer. 23:5; Psa. 23:1; Zech. 9:9-11; 13:6,7; 14:9; John 10:14; Heb. 13:20; Pet. 5:4

Chapter 2

CHRIST,
the Last Adam

GENESIS IS THE BOOK OF GENERATIONS, the history of Adam. The Gospel of Matthew contains the generation of Christ, the son of David, the son of Abraham. In Genesis we find the history of the first Adam. In the Gospel of Matthew we find the last Adam showing His relationship to the Jewish people as Messiah-King.

Adam was a type of Christ in that he was the first of all human beings. From him the race descended. As its federal head Adam fell, bringing down the whole creation with him. Adam was God's first masterpiece, created in perfection and innocence. When he sinned his dominion passed, later to be reinvested in the last Adam, Christ. In creation God formed man. In re-creation He saves man.

Genesis is the book of death; Matthew the book of life. "The *fall* of the first Adam was the *end* of the beginning: the rise of the last Adam was the *beginning* of the end." [1]

In Adam and Christ we have federal heads of two new worlds. Adam was the progenitor and representative of the race. He was the greatest and last work of creation. As such he was physically, mentally, and spiritually complete. He fell from his high estate and thus brought the curse upon his posterity, but by sovereign grace God provided a Redeemer from this curse—the last Adam, Christ Jesus. God said, "The soul that sinneth, it shall die." But the respite came in Christ, the substitute for Adam's sin.

1. Gen. 5:1,2; 1:26; Matt. 1:1

Christ became the world's sacrifice and substitute for sin.

The first Adam was given dominion over all the works of God. These he forfeited through his fall. Now no son of Adam has a right to such universal dominion. Only Christ, the last Adam, can bring order out of chaos. This He will finally accomplish. If man is still in the first Adam, death and judgment are his doom. If in the last Adam, life and blessings will ensue. Adam's apron of fig leaves could not cover his sin. Neither can the works of the flesh. It requires the sacrifice of blood and life. The apron covered only a portion of the body. Self-righteousness and salvation by works cannot cover sin. They are insufficient.

The bone taken from the side of Adam was made a blessing, typifying the relationship of Christ and the believer, made possible by the wounds in Christ's side. In the creation Eve shared the lordship over creation as bone of Adam's bones and flesh of his flesh. Herein is Eve, the bride of Adam, shown to be a type of the bride of the last Adam, Christ. God is revealing the great mystery of our union and oneness with Christ. As the woman was created from man and given his nature, so the believer is created in Christ, given His nature, and made a son of God with Him.[2]

The following contrast can be made between the first and last Adam:

ADAM	CHRIST
Head of the old creation.	The head of the new.[3]
Received the breath of life.	"Breathed on them" the breath of life.[4]
Gave to man a body of flesh, corruptible.	Gives to man a body, incorruptible.[5]
Became a living soul.	Became a "quickening Spirit." [6]
Gave to man a sinful spirit.	Sent to man the Holy Spirit.[7]
Gave the substance from	Will give glorified bodies

2. 1 Cor. 15:45
3. 2 Cor. 5:17
4. Gen. 2:7; John 20:22

5. Rom. 8:1-5; Gen. 6:3; Col. 3:10
6. 1 Cor. 15:45
7. Gal. 6:8; Rom. 7:6

which temporal bodies come.

Links with the earth, earthy.

Was provided with food.

Was the first citizen of the old world.

Was challenged by Satan.

Was tempted in the garden.

Was the chief cornerstone of the old creation.

Was tested by Satan, and fell.

Brought death and destruction.

Was tempted in the physical appetite.

Was tempted to presumption, and sinned.

Was tempted by power and ambition, succumbed.

In sin lost his claim to the old world.

Surrendered God's Word to Satan.

Was ruined by Satan.

Was driven from Paradise in humiliation.

Gives a fallen nature, from below.

Is the old model of man, subject to sin.

when He comes.[8]

Links with the heaven, heavenly.[9]

Suffered for food.[10]

Was the first-born of the new world.[11]

Challenged Satan.[12]

Was tempted in the wilderness.[13]

Is the chief cornerstone of the new creation.[14]

Was tested by Satan, and triumphed.[15]

Brought everlasting life and joy.[16]

Was tempted in the physical appetite.[17]

Was tempted to presumption, without sin.[18]

Was tempted likewise, but overcame.[19]

In death and resurrection proves His claim to the new world.[20]

Resisted Satan with God's Word.[21]

Will eventually ruin Satan.[22]

Will regain Paradise in glorification.[23]

Gives a new nature, from above.[24]

Is the new model for man, perfect and sinless.[25]

8. Gen. 2:23; 1 John 3:2
9. Eph. 4:20,24
10. Gen. 1:29; Matt. 4:2
11. 1 Cor. 15:45; Gen. 1:27; Lu. 1:31
12. Gen. 3:6; Matt. 4:3,4,10
13. Gen. 3:6; Matt. 4:1,5
14. Eph. 2:20
15. Gen. 3:7,8; Matt. 4:11
16. Gen. 2:17; 3:24; John 11:25
17. Gen. 3:6; Matt. 4:2,3

18. Gen. 3:4,11; Matt. 4:3,4
19. Gen. 3:5,12,23; Matt. 4:6,7
20. Gen. 3:17,23; Matt. 28:18; Rev. 21:1
21. Gen. 3:4-6; Matt. 4:4,10
22. Gen. 3:13,19; Rev. 20:2,3,10
23. Gen. 3:23; Rev. 21:2,9
24. Gen. 3:16,24; John 3:3
25. Gen. 4:5; Matt. 5:48; 1 Cor. 15:47

ADAM	CHRIST
Was the first in the insurrection, bringing death.	Is the first in resurrection, bringing life.[26]
Ate of the tree of knowledge, forfeited life.	*Is* the Tree of Life, insuring eternal life.[27]
His first son was a murderer.	Is God's only begotten Son, a Saviour.[28]
His posterity built and lived in man's city.	His followers will live in God's City.[29]
Brought sorrow, pain, tears, and death into the world.	Shall wipe away all tears, sorrow, and death in the world to come.[30]
His home was temporal, marred by sin.	His mansion is eternal, "wherein dwelleth righteousness." [31]
Ruled over the old creation.	Will reign over the new creation.[32]
With his bride was set over the first creation.	With His bride will rule over a redeemed creation.[33]
Took to himself a bride, the woman, who fell.	Will take to Himself a Bride who cannot fall.[34]
Had a bride from his body.	Will have a Bride, which is His body.[35]
His son, Abel, was the first man to slay a typical sacrificial lamb.	*Was* the sacrificial Lamb, "slain before the foundation of the world." [36]
Was tempted by the serpent, the devil.	Will conquer that serpent and cast him into the pit.[37]
His fall was death *to* the race.	Triumphs in life *for* the race.[38]
Was given speech to communicate with God.	Is the Living Word, revealing God.[39]
Was cast from the garden of Eden.	Prayed in the garden of Gethsemane.[40]

26. Rom. 6:23
27. Gen. 3:3,17; Rev. 22:2
28. Gen. 4:8; John 4:42; Matt. 1:21
29. Gen. 4:16,17; Heb. 9:11; 11:10
30. Gen. 3:17-19; Rev. 21:4
31. Gen. 2:8; 4:2,3; John 14:1-3; 2 Peter 3:13
32. Gen. 2:15; 1:26-28; Rev. 11:15; 20:6
33. Gen. 2:16-25; Rev. 20:6
34. Gen. 2:24,25; Eph. 6:23,24
35. Gen. 2:21; Eph. 5:30
36. Gen. 4:4; John 1:36
37. Gen. 3:1-6; Rev. 20:3
38. 1 Cor. 15:22
39. John 1:1
40. John 18:1

Chapter 3

CHRIST,
the Seed

OLD TESTAMENT PROPHECY DID NOT start with the prophetic books, but in Eden. The first Prophet was JEHOVAH-GOD. His first promise announced the virgin birth as the "Seed," the Babe of Bethlehem. Here the miracle of divine incarnation is declared, and also a prophecy of the coming antichrist, the seed of the serpent.

Satan's effort through the ages has been to defeat God's will concerning redemption through this Seed. If it were not for this promised Seed, Adam and Eve would have perished alone; hence, their posterity and their redemption depend upon this Seed.[1]

God said:

I will put enmity between thee and the woman, and between thy seed and her seed; it shall bruise thy head, and thou shalt bruise his heel.

The promise of victory is to the "Seed of the woman," not to the seed of man. In this Seed both Jew and Gentile are to be blessed.[2] The "bruised heel" implies the entire cost of redemption.

With these Old Testament prophecies it is easy to understand the references of the New Testament. However, such passages of the suffering Messiah seemed to have puzzled the Old Testament prophets. Peter says,

1. Gen. 3:15
2. Gen. 12:3; 26:4

But those things, which God before had shewed by the mouth of all his prophets, that Christ should suffer, he hath so fulfilled.

Satan tried to defeat the promise of God in the destruction of this Seed, which often hinged upon the life of one person. In Genesis we have facts regarding Satan explained in figures of speech. The "old serpent," Satan, who tempted the first Adam, was the same Satan who tempted the last Adam, Christ. "Serpent" (Hebrew, *Nachash*) means "shining one." "Thou shalt bruise his heel" refers typically to the sufferings of Christ. "He shall bruise thy head" refers to the final crushing of Satan's purposes, plans, and policies, rather than to the literal crushing of skull and brains.[3] Satan has tried and is still trying to evade the fulfilment of this first prophecy, the carrying out of God's will, in Christ, for His creation. Satan's sphere of activity is antichrist. He is always found fighting on God's ground.[4]

Satan's attack on the Seed can be seen in the slaying of Abel; *"But God"* provided Seth, a third son of Adam. The posterity of Seth began with the "generation of Adam." Seth was born 130 years after the slaying of Abel, and became the substitute for the promised Seed. The other line of the race, the Cainites, had become so corrupt that God was compelled to destroy them. Satan tried to destroy the Seed in the corruption of Seth's posterity. His purpose was to mingle Cain's wicked progeny among Jehovah's people, doubtless the seed of Seth. Satan's method was amalgamation with sinners. God's method is separation from sin. This double line of the Seed has existed, and will exist, until Christ comes the second time as Victor over the devil. The seed of the serpent is every follower of the devil, who in pride and unbelief is exemplified in the person of Cain.

3. Acts 3:18; Rom. 16:20
4. Heb. 2:14; 1 John 3:8; Rev. 20:1-3,10

Eve sinned and caused Adam to do likewise, *"But God"* in grace and mercy caused the woman to be the human agent in bringing the Redeemer into the world. Christ is the Seed. United with Him is His body, the redeemed, of which He is the Head.

In this prophecy of the Seed is the germ of all prophecy relating to the two advents of Christ. In the "bruising of the heel" we have the first coming, Christ's rejection and suffering. In the "bruising of the serpent's head" we have the coming of Christ in power and glory, and finally the destruction of Satan in the "lake of fire." [5]

Because of sin God said:

I will destroy man . . . from the face of the earth. . . .
But Noah found grace in the eyes of the Lord.

In Noah, Shem, and Abraham was the pure Seed of Eve preserved.[6] Five hundred years after the days of Noah, God promised that the Seed was to come through Abraham. Satan is found occupying Canaan in advance of Abraham to destroy the Seed.

According to God's permissive will He allowed a famine to come, and Abraham left for Egypt, forsaking God's promised place of blessing. The promised Seed was in Isaac, yet unborn. In the death of either Abraham or Sarah, Satan would have been victorious. *"But God"* provided the Seed in the son Isaac after Sarah had passed the years of propagation, and Abraham was one hundred years of age.

Through faith also Sarah herself received strength to conceive and was delivered of a child when she was past age.

God performed a biological miracle upon the bodies of Abraham and Sarah when they were passed the age of

5. Gen. 4:1,8; 4:26; 5:1; Isa. 7:14; Matt. 1:23; 23:33
6. Gen. 6:8; 12:4; John 8:44

parenthood. Later, God also preserved Isaac from a similar famine, thus protecting the Seed.[7]

Satan tried to destroy the entire family of the chosen people by famine over all the land. Starvation seemed to be at the door of Jacob and his family, which contained the only remnant of the Seed. Had the line been broken at this point Satan would have won. "*But God*" preserved Joseph in Egypt to save Jacob and Judah, showing His directive will and design.[8]

The fourth famine of testing was in the days of Naomi and Ruth. Famines were one of God's ways of testing.

There was a famine in the land, and a certain man of Bethlehem-Judah went to sojourn in the country of Moab.

God brought forth a beautiful Gentile girl, Ruth, to become the wife of the Jew, Boaz. Ruth became the great-grandmother of David who was the first of the royal Seed.[9]

We have seen Satan's attempt to destroy the male line from the children of Israel. He would now exterminate the entire nation by the oppression and pursuit of Pharaoh. Jacob and his son, Judah, are in Egypt. After the natural death of Jacob, Judah alone is left of the line. "*But God*" preserved Moses as a deliverer: forty years in Egypt, forty years out of Egypt, and forty years leading Israel toward Canaan through the wilderness. "Forty" is the number of "testing." [10]

Again, Satan would have destroyed the nation of Israel at the hand of Haman during their captivity. "*But God*" raised up Queen Esther for their national salvation, and the Seed was preserved.[11]

7. Gen. 12:10-13; 13:4; 26:1-2; Heb. 11:11
8. Gen. 41:56; 47:1
9. Ruth 1:1
10. Gen. 49:33; 50:8; Ex. 1:7-22; 2:5,14; Heb. 11:23
11. Esther 3:6

God promised that the Seed should come through the line of King David. Satan then assaulted the royal Seed and the descendants of David. After attempts to kill King David by the giant Goliath, then by Saul, and afterwards by his son Absalom, Satan watched for a single remaining Seed.[12] This he found in the union of King Jehoram and that wicked heathen wife, Athaliah, the daughter of King Ahab and Jezebel. Jehoram killed his brothers, but had one son to live, Ahaziah. Thus the Seed was preserved. When Ahaziah died his wicked mother, Athaliah, in order to reign, tried to slay all the royal Seed. *"But God"* preserved the little babe, Joash. He was hidden in the temple by his aunt.[13]

The next of the royal Seed depended upon the life of King Hezekiah. He was childless when surrounded by Sennacherib, king of Assyria, in Jerusalem. In those days King Hezekiah was sick unto death and had no heir. It looked as if Satan would be victorious. *"But God"* heard the prayer of Hezekiah and his life was spared for fifteen years, leaving a son twelve years of age. God is faithful.[14]

Satan then sought the true "Seed of the woman," Christ Jesus. He appealed to the fears of Joseph, and would have Mary put away. *"But God"* said to Joseph by the angel of the Lord, "Fear not to take unto thee Mary thy wife." Then Satan put it into the heart of Herod to slay all the innocent babies from two years and younger. *"But God"* warned Joseph and Mary to flee into Egypt.[15]

Satan, seeing that he was defeated, went directly after Christ. At the temptation, Satan said: "Cast thyself down." He misinterpreted the Word of God three times, only to be corrected by Christ. In his consummate conceit, Satan

12. 1 Sam. 16:1-13; 17:31-54; 18:17; 2 Sam. 7:16,17
13. 2 Chron. 17:1; 21:4; 22:10; 23:3; 2 Kings 11:4
14. 2 Kgs. 18 and 19; Isa. 36:1; 38:1-5; Psa. 136
15. Deut. 24:1; Matt. 1:18-20; John 8:3,4; Matt. 2:1-23

thought he could thwart the eternal purposes of God in Christ.[16] Satan would have had the Seed cast down and killed at Nazareth by His own people. Also Satan tried to kill Him by two great storms, and by other means. However, the climax was reached at Calvary. Here the royal Seed, in part "bruised the serpent's head." This promised work of the Seed against Satan will be completely fulfilled at the coming advent of Christ.

The expression, "the seed of the woman," is found only once in the Bible. It is explained in the words of Isaiah,

> Behold, a *virgin* shall conceive, and bear a son, and shall call his name Immanuel [God with us].

Christ was born as Seed of the woman, Seed of Abraham, and Seed of David. As the Seed of the woman He was to bruise the head of Satan; as the Seed of Abraham He was to bring salvation to the household of faith; as the Seed and born into the family of David, He was to fulfil all the Messianic promises. Christ is referred to twelve times in the New Testament as the "Son of David."

By woman sin came; by woman a Saviour is given. Here God's marvelous grace is shown.[17]

16. Matt. 1:16; 2:1-23; Luke 4:1-13; Gen. 3:15
17. Isa. 7:14; Gal. 3:16; Psa. 16; Acts 2:25-36; 13:16-41

Chapter 4

CHRIST
and Satan

MANY REFERENCES TO SATAN AND HIS work are made in the Old Testament. As a deceiver in Eden he came in the form of the serpent and caused Adam and Eve to be driven from the garden. Satan would make God a liar. He caused the second man, Cain, to murder his brother. Satan caused the Seed of the Cainites to corrupt the whole world of that day, with the exception of righteous Noah and his family.

> God saw that the wickedness of man was great in the earth. . . .
> And it repented the Lord that He had made man.

The deluge did not end the wiles of Satan, as we find him entering the home of Noah and making him drunk. He lied as to Job when he said to God:

> Touch his bone and his flesh, and he will curse thee to thy face.
> All that a man hath will he give for his life.

In Jude we read:

> Michael the archangel, when contending with the devil he disputed about the body of Moses, durst not bring against him a railing accusation, but said, The Lord rebuke thee.

Satan caused faithful Abraham and Sarah to lie. He caused the children of Israel to erect the golden calf, and

Aaron and Miriam to murmur against their brother, Moses.
Zechariah records that Joshua had Satan to resist him:

> Joshua the high priest standing before the angel of the
> Lord, and Satan standing at his right hand to resist him.

Satan was responsible for turning Solomon from being
a young man in the favor of God to doing great wickedness
in his latter days. Satan caused Jezebel to kill the prophets,
and Israel to sin. He is today the "prince of the power of the
air," "the god of this age." In his diabolical conceit Satan
will still try to frustrate the purposes of God until cast
into the "lake of fire." Our security against Satan's strate-
gies lies not in our own strength, but in Jehovah's.

> I will be thy shield and thy strong tower.

As to the origin of Satan as recorded in Ezekiel, we find
him pictured as an angelic creation.[1] His fall was before
Adam's creation. He was the "anointed cherub." Lifted up
with pride, he and his angelic followers were cast down.
He was "created perfect in wisdom and beauty." Since his
fall he has been a deceiver as were Achan and Judas.[2] His
audacity is shown in the tempting of Eve,[3] in his withstand-
ing "The angel of the Lord," and in his attack upon the
Christ.[4]

Satan's character is that of a "murderer," a "liar," and an
"accuser." When some spiritual work is to be done we find
Satan personally opposing it. He is a religious devil, usually
found on God's ground. His sphere of operation is in the
religious realm. He questions the truthfulness of God by
doubting His divine Word and substituting his own. Satan
works from without to within in a threefold temptation
by appealing to the bodily senses, "good for food"; to the

1. Ezek. 28:1-19; John 8:44; Gen. 6:5,6; Job 2:5; Zech. 3:1; Jude 9
2. Joshua 7:21; Matt. 26:14
3. Gen. 3:6
4. Zech. 3:2; Rev. 12:7-11; Matt. 4:1

carnal desires, "pleasant to the eyes"; and to the intelligence, "make one wise."

Today, as in the days of our first parents, Satan is attacking saints in the lust of the flesh, "good for food"; the lust of the eyes, "pleasant to the eyes"; and in the pride of life, "make one wise." [5] In egotism Satan says:

I will ascend (in ascension).
I will exalt (in exaltation).
I will sit (in glorification).

But his doom is foretold. "I will cast thee . . . out . . . I will . . . bring forth a fire . . . and never shalt thou be any more." [6]

As a deceiver Satan's counterfeits are not wholly false. He mixes truth and error to give credibility, in order to deceive "the very elect." Satan perverts and distorts the gospel. In 1 John 4:1-3, Scripture furnishes the method of testing the false doctrines of Satan. He cannot supplant the truth with a lie, hence he adulterates it with error.

When Jesus and Satan met in the wilderness, at the end of Jesus' forty days' fasting, Satan tested Him with the philosophy of life based on self-preservation through one's own self-sufficiency. The test has a twofold implication: First, You have power (self-sufficiency). Power is self-preservation. Secondly, You do not need faith in or dependence on anything, or anybody. It was primarily an effort of Satan to break down the faith of Jesus so that He would misuse or abuse His power. That has been humanity's ruin. Satan would turn faith into fanaticism, and prostitute power. To abandon faith is the satanic philosophy of life. Jesus enumerated His law of life to Peter, saying:

Whosoever will come after Me, let him deny himself, and take up his cross, and follow Me. For whosoever

5. Gen. 3:6; Is. 14:13
6. Ezek. 28:16-19

will save his life shall lose it; but whosoever shall lose his life for My sake and the gospel's, the same shall save it.

Satan would minimize sin, humanize God, and deify man.

The Bible clearly differentiates between the work of Christ and that of Satan:[7]

CHRIST	SATAN
Came in the Father's name.	Came in his own name.
Came from above.	Came from beneath.
Did the Father's will.	Did only his own will.
Glorified the Father.	Blasphemes the Father.
In the flesh was humble.	Is self-exalted.
Came to save.	Comes to destroy.
Brings peace.	Brings desolation.
Takes His own to Heaven.	Leads his own to hell.
Has His children.	Has his children.
Has His servants.	Has his servants.
Has His kingdom.	Is "the god of this age."
Has His habitation.	Is the "prince of the power of the air."
Has His ministers.	His ministers are "transformed as ministers of righteousness."
Has His doctrines.	Has the "doctrines of demons."
Has His angels.	Has the "devil and his angels."
Has His Church.	Has his "synagogue of Satan."
Brings life.	His wages are "sin and death."
Brings eternal light.	Brings eternal darkness.
Made man in God's image.	Proposes that men be as gods.

7. John 8:12,44; Rom. 6:11,22; Mark 8:34,35; Eph. 2:2,3; Rev. 20:11-15; 2 Cor. 4:4; 11:15; 1 Tim. 4:1; Matt. 25:41; 27:25

CHRIST	SATAN
Gives to man an Eden.	Would have man produce his own Eden.
Would give freedom *from* sin.	Gives liberty *to* sin.
Gives to the believer a new nature.	Gave to man a fallen nature.

Chapter 5

CHRIST
"The Angel of the Lord"
(Hebrew, *Malach-Jehovah*)

CHRIST APPEARS IN THE PATRIARCHAL, Mosaic, and Christian dispensations as JEHOVAH (the Word of God) revealing the Father to man, and carrying forward God's plan of redemption. He is also referred to as "Mine Angel," "Angel of God," and "Angel of the Lord." [1]

In the Old Testament there are appearances of a supernatural Being who is called "The Angel of Jehovah." He is identified with JEHOVAH (YAVEH) and speaks of Himself as "I AM the God of Bethel." "The Angel [messenger, or one sent] of the Lord [JEHOVAH]" implies a distinction in the Godhead. The Father is never sent but always sends. The Angel seems to be the preincarnate Christ—a "Christophany" (appearance of Christ)—and walked with Adam in the garden. He has the same description as Christ, accepts worship due to God, appears in human form, out of the fire, out of heaven, "the mysterious visitant."

JEHOVAH-CHRIST, as "The Angel of the Lord," appeared unto Abraham at the great testing time of his life in the offering of Isaac. Also, in the form of a man when the "three men stood by him" on the plains of Mamre announcing that Isaac was to be born. There He not only conversed, but ate with Abraham. The Angel of the Lord said to Joshua at Jericho,

1. Gen. 16:7-13; 31:11-13; 48:15,16; Judges 6:20-24; 13:3; Isa. 63:8-10; Ex. 16:7-14; 23:20-23; 33:14,15; 32:34; 14:19; 2 Sam. 14:17,20; Heb. 1:3

The place whereon thou standest is holy [ground].

He announced, as "captain of the host of the Lord am I now come." He stood beside Joshua to strengthen him, who reverenced Him as a divine being.[2]

He was typified by Melchisedec, King of righteousness, "the priest of the Most High God," who met Abraham as he returned from the slaughter of the kings and offered him bread and wine, and blessed him and received tithes of him.

The Angel of the Lord appeared unto Hagar in the wilderness. This bondwoman of Abraham recognized the Angel of the Lord as the One sent, a messenger. The Angel wrestled with Jacob at Peniel ("the face of God") and blessed him. He spoke to Moses at the burning bush, and was the great I AM.[3] He led the children of Israel from Egypt to Canaan. He caused the ass to save Balaam. He used Gideon in delivering his people. He appeared unto Manoah and wife, the mother of Samson, and afterward ascended to heaven in the flame of the altar before their eyes.[4] He was with David at the threshing floor when David confessed his sin. He was with Elijah under the juniper tree. He was with Daniel in the lions' den, and with the Hebrew children in the fiery furnace. Thus the angel foreshadowed Christ in His office of Redeemer and Saviour.[5]

The function of the Angel of the Lord was as "The Lord of the Harvest," the One to do the Lord's business. He was the ministering One "in righteousness" to Elijah, and "the Deliverer." [6] It was the Angel of the Lord that directed

2. Gen. 22:11-18; 18:2,22; 19:1,17; Josh. 5:13-15
3. Gen. 16:7-11; 21:17; 28:12; 14:18; 31:11; 32:24-30; 48:16; Hosea 12:4; Ex. 3:2,14; 23:20; 32:34
4. Ex. 14:10; Judges 2:1-4; Num. 22:22-35; Judges 6:11-22; 13:2,3,20
5. 1 Kgs. 19:5-11; Dan. 6:22; 8:16; 9:21; 10:5; 12:5-7; 3:25,28; 2 Sam. 24:16; 1 Chron. 21:12,15-18
6. Gen. 16:7,13; 24:40; 1 Kgs. 19:7; 2 Kgs. 1:3; Psa. 34:7; 35:5,6; Zech. 12:8

Philip in his journey, who spoke to Cornelius, and who ministered unto Paul and Peter. He will some day act in Judgment. He it was whom John saw from the Isle of Patmos.[7]

The Angel of the Lord is the same as the uncreated Angel of the Covenant referred to in Malachi, and also in the Revelation, as removing Satan from the earth. Christ's being designated as "Angel" connects Him with the Covenant and with God's earthly people, Israel.

JEHOVAH-CHRIST was made "lower than the angels" for the suffering of death, that He might be made higher than the angels in His inheritance in the saints and in His exaltation.

Isaiah saw the vision of the seraphim as they cried, "Holy, holy, holy, is Jehovah of hosts: the whole earth is full of His glory." No angel or archangel could have become Redeemer. "The chariots of God are twenty thousand, even thousands of angels; Jehovah is among them." The angels of God in Old Testament times were quick in obedience, and the Angel of the Lord was among them, not one of them.

There are also celestial spirits referred to in the Scriptures as ordinary angels, "an angel." They are created and immortal. These angels are of different orders. They worship God, and are not to be worshiped. They do not marry, and are obedient unto God. They are ministering spirits, but not equals of the Angel of the Lord.[8]

7. Acts 8:26,29; 10:7,19,30; 5:19; 27:23,24; 12:7; 2 Kgs. 19:35; Isa. 37:36
8. Gen. 2:1; Neh. 9:6; Col. 1:16; Luke 20:36; Isa. 6:2; 1 Thess. 4:16; Jude 9; Phil. 2:9; Psa. 148:2; Col. 2:8; Rev. 19:10; Matt. 22:30; Mark 12:25; 6:10; Luke 11:2; Psa. 103:20; Psa. 8:5; Heb. 1:4; 2:7,9,16

Chapter 6

CHRIST
and the Tabernacle

TYPES, SYMBOLS, FIGURES OF SPEECH, AND shadows of the real illustrate some truths of the divine antitype of Christ. Figures of speech give the *form* in which the words are used, taken out of their ordinary sense for the purpose of emphasis. For true interpretation the reader should avoid taking literally that which is figurative, or taking figuratively that which is literal. Paul plainly states that these types and symbols are given for examples, for learning, and for profit. No type is perfect.

> All these things happened unto them for ensamples
> [types]: . . . for our admonition.

The person, work, and glory of Christ are the substance of the Old Testament types. To know Him better we must know them. Jesus said, "Moses wrote of Me."

The book of Exodus is the history of Israel, emerging from slavery into a nation. It is the book of redemption and sets forth the need of a lost race. The symbolism in Exodus shows Israel in bondage to Pharaoh, a type of the believer in bondage to Satan. Israel's wilderness wanderings present a sad picture of a defeated Christian, finally reaching the goal.[1] Exodus is rich in typical teachings. Salvation by Christ's blood and His work of redemption from the guilt and power of sin are foreshadowed. This is seen in the

1. Psa. 29:9; Ex. 25:40; 1:1-11; 1 Cor. 10:11

destruction of the Egyptians, and in Israel's passover. For four hundred years the children of Israel were in bondage. They increased in number from about seventy souls in the family of Jacob to about two million at the time of deliverance. Israel (Jacob) entered Egypt as a large family. They left it as a nation.

The Egyptians were a type of the unbelieving world. God was determined to deliver His people from their oppression. He has always desired a separated people and has provided a Canaan-life for them.[2] JEHOVAH-CHRIST wanted to dwell among His people. He gave the pattern of the Tabernacle to Moses. Fifteen hundred years thereafter, Christ was to come as God manifest in the flesh—in incarnation.[3]

The Tabernacle of the Old Testament is a beautiful picture and type of the person, work, and glory of JEHOVAH-CHRIST. It speaks of the Christ-life on earth, and of His dwelling place in its different appointments and priesthood teachings.[4] The psalmist says, "In His temple doth every one speak of His glory." Every part of the Tabernacle proclaims the glory of Christ in some way.

In the building of the Tabernacle, Jehovah desired the freewill offerings of His people.[5] The same applies to His followers today. There was no Tabernacle debt. They were not to go down into Egypt (a type of the world) for help. These Israelites were not only willing to bring their "tithes into the storehouse of the Lord," but they brought also an additional freewill offering.[6]

In the description of the Tabernacle, the record begins with God in the "most holy place." God could meet man at the brazen altar of sacrifice, but sinful man could not

2. Heb. 11:26; 2 Cor. 6:17
3. Ex. 25:8; 2 Chron. 3:3; 1 Cor. 3:9; 2 Cor. 5:1; John 1:1,14
4. Heb. 9:1-24; 1 Cor. 10:1-11
5. Ex. 25:1,2; 35:4,5,20-22,29; 2 Cor. 8:12; Eph. 2:21,22
6. Ex. 36:5-7; Mal. 3:8-10; Mark 16:15; 2 Cor. 9:7

meet God in the "holy of holies." Man can only meet God at the Cross, and then as a believer-priest enter the most holy place.[7]

The *outer court* of the Tabernacle was 50 cubits wide and 100 cubits long, with 60 pillars, 20 at the south, 20 at the north, 10 at the west, and 10 at the east, 5 cubits apart. These pillars were of wood, covered with brass, with sockets and pins of brass. The brass of the outer court was a symbol of judgment, as will be seen later.

The *hangings* of white around the outer court were of fine twined linen, 6 cubits high, a symbol of the holiness and righteousness of Christ. He alone could atone for the sin of the world, and become the Passover Lamb. Perfection of the saints can only be found in Him, the perfect One. Even His enemies declared Him sinless.[8] As the fine twined linen was a thing of the earth, with its processes of death and resurrection, so was the incarnate Christ in death, burial, and resurrection.

The *gate* of the Tabernacle was the only way to enter the outer court and to get to God in the most holy place. This is a picture of man's approach to God. He must first meet God at the appointed place: "I AM The Door." [9]

The plan of salvation originated in the love of God. The sinner is told to repent of his sin, believe, and receive Christ as a personal Saviour. Christ, then, becomes the procuring cause of salvation in His sacrifice on Calvary. The gate, like the door of Noah's Ark, is a type of the heavenly Door, Christ, opening His bountiful storehouse for believers. The east gate, facing the sunrise, tells of that day when Christ shall arise as the "Sun of righteousness with healing in His wings." [10]

7. Heb. 9:12

8. Ex. 27:9,10,18; John 8:46; Matt. 27:4,54; 1 Pet. 2:22-24; Rev. 19:8

9. Ex. 38:18; John 10:9; 14:6; Acts 4:12; Heb. 7:25; Titus 3:5; Psa. 40:2; 1 John 4:10

10. Psa. 78:23; John 10:9; Rev. 3:20; Gen. 3:24

The four *colors* of the gate are significant, and are types of four aspects in the life of Christ: *white* symbolizes the stainless, sinless, spotless holiness and purity of Christ. *Blue* symbolizes the heavenly relationship of Christ. *Purple* symbolizes the royalty and kingliness of Christ. *Scarlet* symbolizes the earthly glory and sufferings of Christ, and His ability to save from the penalty, power, and dominion of sin by the shedding of His blood, satisfying divine justice.[11] In these four colors we have the four aspects of the character of Christ in the Gospels:

Matthew—*purple*—Christ as King of the Jews, ruling.
"Behold, thy King cometh unto thee."
Mark—*scarlet*—Christ as Servant, humbly dying on the cross.
"Behold, My servant whom I uphold."
Luke—*white*—Christ as the stainless Son of man, in humility. (Christ is mentioned as the Son of man seventy-seven times in the New Testament.)
"Behold, the Man, whose name is The Branch."
John—*blue*—Christ in Deity, as the co-existent Son of God.
"Behold, your God." [12]

The *brazen altar* was 3 cubits high, and 5 cubits in length and width. Here the burnt-offering, the memorials of the meat-offering, the peace-offering, and the fat of the sin-offering were burned. The flesh, bones, and the skin of the sin-offering were burnt to ashes on the earth outside the camp, quite a distance away. The ground was wet with blood all about the altar where the horned animals were slain. Here the sins of the sinner are transferred to the innocent sacrificial animal, typical of Christ, who suffered "the just for the unjust." God values the sinner saved by grace according to the value of the offering, which is Christ. Here Christ is a type in reconciliation, justification, and

11. Ex. 26:1; 27:16; 1 Pet. 2:22; Jer. 23:6; Ex. 28:28; John 3:13; 18:37; Psa. 72; Luke 1:32,33; Rev. 19:13; Psa. 22:6,14,15; John 19:30
12. Zech. 9:9; Isa. 42:1; Zech. 6:12; Isa. 40:9

salvation, where the sinner is saved from the penalty of sin.

The altar was of acacia wood, completely covered with brass (copper). Brass is a composite metal, produced through fire. Brass points to the judgment of Christ. Wood is a type of the humanity of Christ. The "horns of the altar" are symbolic of power, strength, and might; pointing to the power, safety, and the universality of Christ's sacrifice.[13]

Without shedding of blood there is no remission for sin.

The *offering* laid on the brass altar typifies Christ. It could be brought by the sinner to the priest, and consisted of a bullock (ox), lamb, he-goat, turtle-dove, or young pigeon. God meets the sinner at the altar of brass (judgment) in the person of His Son, crucified. This satisfied divine justice. The sinner must appear at the brass altar either in judgment or in the substitutionary, sacrificial work of his offering, Christ Jesus.

The *ashes* left from the burnt-offering were carefully taken to a "clean place." These ashes were typical of the body of Christ, tenderly taken to the clean, undefiled resting-place in Joseph's new tomb.

At the brass altar Christ is found as coming, "Not to be ministered unto, but to minister, and to give His life a ransom for many." It is at the brass altar that the sinner is "born again." As in the red heifer offering, the sinner was cleansed by water, but in the water were the ashes of the red heifer. The *standing* or *position* of the believer in justification is to be found in the brass altar. His *state* or *condition* is to be found in sanctification at the brass laver.[14]

Brass and *silver* were the metals used outside the Tabernacle. Gold only was used on the inside. Brass symbolizes righteous judgment and power under the protection of

13. Ex. 27:1-6; 1 Sam. 2:10; Psa. 89:17; Jer. 48:25; Heb. 9:22; 1 John 1:9; Isa. 45:22; 1 Kgs. 1:50-53; Lev. 1:6-9; 4:12; 16:27; 1 Pet. 3:18; 2:24; Isa. 53:5,6; John 1:29
14. Matt. 20:28; Isa. 64:6; 61:10; 1 Pet. 1:23; John 3:3,5; Num. 19:17; John 19:34; 1 John 5:6; 2 Cor. 5:17; John 15:4,5; Gal. 2:20

Christ. The sinner, not able to pay the penalty for sin (death), could bring a substitute to die in his place, typifying Christ, the Substitute, on the cross.[15]

The Hebrew word, "serpent" in Genesis is *Nachash*, meaning a "shining one." In Chaldee it means copper, or brass, because it shines. In Isaiah it means "a burning one." In Numbers the serpent on the pole was burning because of the poison in its bite.

Satan is spoken of as "an angel of light," a beautiful, shining angelic personality, possessor of great knowledge and superiority. Ezekiel gives a picture of Satan, from his origin to final doom, under the type of the "prince of Tyre." In the book of Numbers a threefold lesson is taught in the raising of the brass serpent, which symbolizes Christ upon the Cross, taking upon Himself the sin of the world.

Punishment—"Sent fiery serpents."
Perishing—"Much people . . . died."
Provision—"Serpent . . . upon a pole." [16]

The brass laver. Before the priest could enter the holy place of the Tabernacle to do his service, his hands and feet had to be cleansed daily at the brass laver. Typically, water is for cleansing from all defilement, and it is a type of the living Word of God. The laver is not for sins before conversion, but afterward. The altar comes before the laver. If salvation and justification are at the altar, sanctification and preservation are continued at the laver.

Be ye clean, that bear the vessels of the Lord.[17]

There were no dimensions given for the brass laver. There are none for the cleansing power of Christ. The believer's

---

15. Rom. 5:21; Num. 21:6-9; John 3:14,15; Rev. 1:15
16. Gen. 3:15; Matt. 16:23; Isa. 6:2,6; 2 Cor. 11:3,4; Ezek. 28:1-19; Isa. 14:12-14; Rev. 20:10; Num. 21:8
17. Ex. 30:17-20; 40:7; Titus 3:5; Isa. 52:11; Eph. 5:25,26; John 17:17; Eccl. 9:8; Heb. 12:14; 1 John 1:7; Ex. 38:8; John 3:5; Psa. 24:3,4

judicial or objective sanctification began in regeneration at the brass altar, and continued, subjectively, at the laver. It will end in the sanctification of character when he meets his glorified Sanctifier in the most holy place.[18]

The preservation of the believer in Christ is clearly shown at the laver. Here provision was made for his daily cleansing of exposed parts. In the thirteenth chapter of John three different Greek words are used. Peter says to his Lord, "Thou shalt never wash [*nipto*] my feet." Jesus answers, "If I wash [*nipto*, meaning to wash some part of the body] thee not, thou hast no part [fellowship] with Me." Peter saith unto Him, "Lord, not my feet only, but also my hands and head." Then it is that Jesus uses another Greek word:

> He that is washed [*louo*, meaning to bathe the whole body] needeth not save to wash [*nipto*] his feet, but is clean [Greek, *katharos*] every whit: and ye are clean, but not all ("all" referring to Judas).

The exposed parts of the priest would contact defilement and required cleansing, but not his covered body. That was judicial and objective cleansing, once for all. The blood of Christ covers the believer's *guilt*, but he needs cleansing from constant daily defilement. Aaron, the first high priest, had been thoroughly washed by Moses from head to foot at the gate of the Tabernacle, and had been clothed in a spotless robe. He was then in a position to proceed toward the laver. Likewise the sinner is cleansed and clothed in the righteousness of Christ before he can approach the Father in the most holy place. "The blood of Jesus Christ," shed once for all, continues to keep the believer clean.[19]

Wood and metals. Before entering the Tabernacle, notice the wood and metals with their typical meanings. The acacia

18. Jude 24,25; Ezek. 36:25-27; Acts 15:8,9; Heb. 6:1
19. 1 John 1:1-10; Psa. 51:7; John 10:28; 13:8-10; Heb. 10:1-12

wood is a type of the humanity of Christ. The wood is said by some to be the same as that of the "burning bush" which Moses saw, and was enduring.[20]

As has been indicated, brass stands as a type of strength, power, and judgment of the coming Christ-Judge.

Silver is the type of redemption or ransom, and was the redemptive money. An Israelite at the age of twenty had to give a half-shekel of silver as a ransom, or atonement, for his soul. Without this he could not become a part of the family of Israel. Hence, the redemptive money. The rich could not bring more, nor the poor less. All were upon the same level as to redemption. The believer's redemption is purchased by the precious blood of Christ of which silver is a type. The silver-socket foundation of redemption will hold, for the believer is saved and made safe through the redeeming blood of Calvary.[21]

If wood is a type of the humanity of Christ, brass symbolizing His power and strength in judgment, and silver the foundation price of redemption, then all must find its center in *gold*—type of the deity and holiness of Jehovah. Isaiah says, "I will make a man more precious than fine gold." In Exodus we read, "Thou shalt make forty sockets of silver under the twenty boards." There were forty-eight boards in the Tabernacle. These boards were covered with pure gold, sunken deeply into the silver-socket foundation for strength to stand. Hence, we find the deity and redemptive work of Jehovah blended together in the salvation of the lost.[22] The candlestick and mercy seat were also of pure gold, and all of the wood in the Tabernacle was covered with the same. No other metals were seen. Gold is not only a type of the deity and holiness of Christ, but also of His glory.

20. John 1:42; Acts 13:9; Phil. 4:13
21. Ex. 27:17; 30:12-16; 1 Pet. 1:18,19; 2 Tim. 1:12; Matt. 5:24; Jude 24; Mal. 3:3
22. Isa. 13:12; Ex. 26:15-29

It represents Calvary, where Christ was offered as a "sweet-smelling incense." The golden branches of the candlestick were not exempt from suffering. They were *beaten* of one piece of pure gold. Deity must have suffered in Christ.[23] Gold displays the beauty of the Bridegroom to His bride. Solomon says, "His legs are as pillars of marble, set upon sockets of fine gold." As gold is a type of deity, holiness, glory, and kingliness of Christ, so frankincense typifies His perfect life. Myrrh (meaning "crushed") typifies His suffering.

The Tabernacle is 10 by 30 cubits with its two rooms, placed within the court, separated from the defilement without. The 48 boards, fitting closely, were covered with gold. The ceiling was of ten curtains, marvelously wrought, with figures of heavenly creatures embroidered thereon. The two rooms, or apartments, of the Tabernacle were called the "holy place" and the "holy of holies"; the first being 10 by 20 cubits and the last 10 by 10 cubits. The cloud by day and the pillar of fire by night directed the movements of the camp and the Tabernacle. This was the Shekinah glory of JEHOVAH-CHRIST. He, being the antitype of the cloud, guides and protects His children by day and by night, according to His directive will.[24]

The *curtains*, or coverings, for the Tabernacle (or tent) were of ram's skin, dyed red, and the outer covering was of badger's skin. The Greek Septuagint translates the Hebrew word for badger's skin, "skins of blue leather," out of which shoes were made. This outer covering was all that was seen by the Israelites, and they never saw the beauty of the interior. Thus the badger skin typified the humanity of Christ.[25] The ram's skins, dyed red, were beneath the badger's skin. The ram was a type of Christ, pointing to Calvary.

23. Ex. 25:31; 30:1-3; Zech. 4:2-6; Isa. 53:5; Luke 24:26; Heb. 2:10; 5:8; Phil. 3:10; Heb. 4:15
24. Ex. 26:1-6,14; 40:36,37; 13:21; Num. 9:15-23; Psa. 105:39; S. of S. 5:15
25. Isa. 53:2; Ezek. 16:10; Eph. 2:20,21; Lev. 16:4; Matt. 20:28; Luke 9:58; Phil. 2:7; Isa. 60; Heb. 1:3; John 8:12; Lev. 8:24; Gen. 22:15,16

The Tabernacle is a type of Christ in His twofold nature, human and divine. We cannot fathom the mystery of His incarnation, but we can believe it. The boards closely fastened together typify how all believers are one in Christ. The acacia wood, of which these boards were made, was found in the desert. The tree had to be cut down and die (as did Christ), for it to become of value in salvation.

Resting in the silver sockets of redemption, the boards became a type of the humanity in the redemptive work of Christ, covered with the gold of His deity. "In death He agonized, rising He justifies, coming He glorifies." The acacia wood had to be removed from the desert to become pillars for the Lord. Such a choice from the desert is but a type of the elective love of Jehovah, now gathering out His elect from the sinful nations of earth.[26]

The goat's hair, covering the ram's skin, was white, perhaps from the white Angora goats of Palestine. There was no black (the type of sin) connected with the Tabernacle. A goat was used as a sin-offering at the great Jewish feasts, a lesson of substitution, pointing to the Passover and Pentecost. Christ is the believers' sin-offering. As High Priest He brings the blood from the brazen altar and sprinkles it on the mercy seat within the most holy place, making atonement for sin. The high priest laid both hands upon the head of the goat and turned him loose in the wilderness, never to return with the sins of Israel. Symbolically, Israel's sins were upon the goat. Thus he became Israel's Scapegoat, as Christ becomes the substitute for the believer.[27]

The golden candlestick was made of one beaten piece of pure gold, the cost of which was "one talent," valued at about $30,000. It had seven lights, and was the only light in

26. Isa. 53:2; Eph. 2:19,20; John 17:20,21; Psa. 133:1-3; Acts 15:13-17; Eph. 1:4; 1 Pet. 1:2
27. Ex. 26:7,9; 23:19; 1 Cor. 15:23; John 14:19; Heb. 12:23; 1 Tim. 2:5; Rom. 4:5; Psa. 103:12; Isa. 38:17; Micah 7:19

the Tabernacle. It consisted of six branches and one main shaft. Six is the number of incompleteness (the number of man) as seven is the number of completeness. Perfection is symbolized in the golden candlestick, as the believer's perfection is found in Christ.

In the golden candlestick were four bowls with almonds, knops, and flowers. This is a beautiful type of Christ in fruitfulness and His union with believers. The tall center shaft speaks of Christ, the Vine, while the almonds, knops, and flowers represent the fruits of His labors in close relationship. The golden candlestick ("light-bearer") is a type of Christ, the Illuminator, the Light which can never be extinguished. He is "the Light of the world" and the Author of Light.[28]

Light was the first creation of the natural world, earth's chiefest glory, JEHOVAH-CHRIST clothing nature with beauty. Greater is Christ in His Shekinah light and glory. As the Creator is greater than His creation, so the Light from heaven excels His lower lights of earth. "The Light" was the life of the world, opening the eyes of the blind, giving a vision of salvation to the woman at the well, and illuminating the poor publican crying for salvation. The Light caused multitudes to see Lazarus raised from the dead, and changed Thomas from a life of doubt. He will give light, life, and liberty to all who believe and receive Him as Saviour.

Christ is the *Source* of Light—Light for us.
Christ is the *Spirit* of Light—Light in us.
Christ is the *Shining* Light—Light through us.

No natural light was needed in the most holy place. It was illumined by the Shekinah glory and presence of Je-

28. Ex. 25:31-37; Zech. 4:2-6; Rev. 1:12,20; Isa. 60:19; Heb. 1:3; John 10:27; 2 Tim. 1:12; 1 Pet. 1:5; Gal. 3:28; John 15:5; 17:23; 1 Cor. 12:12; John 8:12; Ex. 27:20; Prov. 4:18; Matt. 5:14

hovah-Light. The "candle" in the book of Job is a type of the light of Christ, who cares for and comforts His own:

When his candle shined upon my head, and when by his light I walked through darkness.

The *oil* was constantly placed in the golden candlestick as a symbol of the spirit of Christ in joy within the life of the true believer.[29]

The *golden table of shewbread* was 2 cubits long, 1 cubit broad, and 1½ cubits high. It was made of acacia wood, covered with pure gold. Twelve loaves of bread were placed thereon, remaining as an offering to God for one week and were then eaten by the priests in the holy place. The table was never empty (a divine provision), and the bread was made of the finest flour.

In the golden table of shewbread we have a beautiful type of Christ as the believers' Sustainer, the "Bread of Life." He is the "manna" from heaven, coming down to be beaten and crushed in order to become the Provider and Sustainer of life, sweet to the taste of the believer. Christ in incarnation was the unleavened bread in perfection. The "loaves" were a type of death and resurrection; the wheat in the bread must die, be crushed, and raised to bring forth life from the dead. The "manna" in the Ark of the Covenant did not spoil. It was typical of the incorruptible Bread of Life, and a reminder to future generations.[30]

In Amos we have a type of famine for the Word of God, which is so prevalent today:[31]

Behold, the days come, saith the Lord God, that I will send a famine in the land, not a famine of bread,

29. Gen. 1:16; John 8:12; 1 John 4:13; Matt. 5:14; Job 29:3
30. Ex. 25:23-30; 16:13,31; 12:8; Luke 14:17; 15:17; John 6:33-36,53; Isa. 58:11; Psa. 23:5; 133:1
31. Amos 8:11; John 6:32,35,51

nor a thirst for water, but of hearing the words of the Lord.

In John's Gospel Christ is offering Himself in a threefold manner:

True bread from heaven—Satisfying.
I Am the Bread of Life—Sustaining.
I Am the Living Bread—Substituting.

The golden altar of incense was foursquare, 1 cubit long and broad, and 2 cubits high. It was made of acacia wood, covered with pure gold, signifying the twofold nature of Christ, human and divine. Here we find Christ our Intercessor, meeting the need of His people in intercessory prayer. The incense was burned with fire from the brazen altar which never went out. The sweet spices and frankincense are typical of the perfection, completeness, and beauty as found in the Christ-Intercessor. King Solomon typifies the beauties of Christ as "the Lily of the valleys," "the Rose of Sharon," and "Altogether Lovely." [32]

The *incense* was to be offered only by those of the Aaronic priesthood. Any "strange fire" placed thereon meant certain death. Nadab and Abihu, sons of Aaron, were slain for bringing strange fire. Uzziah, king of Judah, was a faithful king during the first part of his reign. Afterwards presuming to offer incense upon the golden altar, he was smitten with leprosy which continued until his death. [33]

As Christ showed His dependence upon the Father in prayer at the time of need, so believers today need to remain near the altar of prayer, the golden altar of incense. [34]

The placing of all the furniture in the outer court and in the holy place form a perfect *cross*. This did not just happen, but was in the plan of God.

32. Ex. 30:1-6; John 1:14; 14:13,14; 16:23; 17; Psa. 141:1,2; Rev. 5:8
33. Lev. 10:1,2; 2 Chron. 26:16-23; 2 Kgs. 15:1-7
34. Psa. 22:10; 45:8; 1 Pet. 5:7

A *veil* separated the holy place from the holy of holies, known as the inner veil. The high priest could only lift the corner of the veil and enter this most holy place once a year on the Day of Atonement. Christ, in death, rent this veil, and made possible the sinner's presence before God. It is a type of the body of Christ.[35]

The *Ark of the covenant* was made of acacia wood, overlaid within and without with pure gold. It was placed within the holy of holies. JEHOVAH demanded the building of the Tabernacle, "That I might dwell among them." He was to abide amid Shekinah glory in the most holy place, above the golden blood-sprinkled mercy-seat.

The Ark was to guide Israel in her forty-year pilgrimage, going before the people in search of a resting place. The Ark was for the wilderness journey, and eventually to find its permanency in the Temple.[36] In the Ark were the two tables of the law, a pot of manna, and Aaron's rod. Atonement was completd by Christ on the Cross when He cried, "It is finished." The manna typifies Christ as Provider, and the budding rod of Aaron symbolizes Christ in resurrection. Only tables of the law were in the Ark when placed in Solomon's Temple.[37]

Again the twofold nature of Christ is seen in the Ark: the wood a type of His humanity, and the gold a type of His deity; both of which meet the sinner, in grace, at the blood-sprinkled mercy-seat.

The Ark is also typical of the believers' resting-place in Christ. As the Ark was in the center of the most holy place, so Christ's presence is in the midst of His people.

Two golden cherubim were fastened to the mercy-seat, between which was the Shekinah fire, a token of His pres-

35. Ex. 26:31-35; Matt. 26:26; 27:51; Heb. 10:20
36. Ex. 25:10-21; 33:14,15,40; Num. 10:33; Isa. 45:2; Josh. 3:15, 16; John 10:4
37. John 19:30; Psa. 40:8; 80:8; Rom. 10:4; Phil. 2:8; Num. 17:8,10

ence and typifying the throne of God.[38] These cherubim were celestial, spirit-beings, associated with the mercy-seat. They were to preserve, keep, and guard. They were beautifully embroidered upon the veil, representing the incarnation and redemption of Christ.[39]

Comparison can be made between the Old Testament Tabernacle and the life of Christ, as follows:

TABERNACLE	CHRIST
A temporary appointment, on the move, remaining briefly.	In the flesh-life, temporary, about thirty-three years on the earth.
For use in the wilderness amid hardship and sufferings.	Came to a wilderness life; born in a manger, no home, and a borrowed grave.
Outwardly unattractive, badger skin, and glory hidden.	Glory hidden behind His flesh, His visage marred.
God's dwelling place, the curtain separating it.	Becoming flesh, God dwells in the Person of Christ.
Where God meets man, the sinner, at the gate.	Spans the gulf between God and man.
Was in the center of Israel's camp, the meeting place.	Is the gathering place of the redeemed, now and hereafter.
Was where the law of God was preserved.	Was preserving the law by fulfilling it.
Was where sacrifices were made.	Became the Sacrifice, Passover, and expiator.
Was the place where the priestly family was fed.	Is the spiritual food for God's priestly family.
Was the place of worship, through which all sacrifices came.	Is the only sacrificial source through which we get to God.[40]

38. Rom. 3:24,25; Heb. 4:16; 1 John 4:10; Ex. 25:17-22; Matt. 11:28
39. Ex. 28:18,23; Gen. 3:24; Heb. 10:10,20
40. John 1:14; Ex. 25:21,22; John 14:6; 1 Tim. 2:5; Deut. 10:2; Psa. 40:7,8; Lev. 6:16,26; 1 Pet. 2:5; Heb. 13:15

Chapter 7

CHRIST
the Paschal Lamb

IN THE BEGINNING GOD PROVIDED FOR salvation. The slain Lamb "was foreordained before the foundation of the world," and the believer was "chosen in Him [Christ]." After man fell into sin, the blood of animals was shed. This introduced a blood sacrifice for the remission of sin, looking forward to Calvary and the sacrifice of God's Lamb for the sin of the world. Later this was perverted by certain ancient peoples, bringing about the horrible system of human sacrifices in religious ceremonies.

The whole plan of redemption was in the mind of God before the foundation of the world, originating in God's great love for His creation. No afterthought, no surprises, no mistakes with God. He counted the thing that was not as though it was. The shed blood of the Lamb was a part of the original plan of salvation in the eternal past: "According as He hath chosen us in Him before the foundation of the world." Where there is no sin, there is no need of a sacrificial Lamb. Sin necessitated His mediatorial service. Long before Calvary became a fact, it was purposed by God. Christ was "the Lamb slain from the foundation of the world."

When Israel was spending her last night in Egypt, the plague of death was to be visited upon the people. The death-angel was to pass through and the first-born of every home to die, unless provision had been met for his safety. An innocent lamb, in its first year, without spot or blemish, was to be slain, and its blood sprinkled with hyssop upon the doorposts and lintel of each home. When the death-angel came at midnight, such were to be spared.[1]

The Passover is a type of God's plan of redemption, pointing to Christ "The Lamb of God, which taketh away the sin of the world." Prophetically, the "Lamb [that hath been] slain from the foundation of the world." The Passover was the Old Covenant picture of Calvary. Either the lamb had to die, or the first-born.

Christ only could become the Sin-bearer of the world, and must die as a Lamb "without spot or blemish," being made sin for the sinner; thus He credited to the sinner His righteousness, and charged the believers' sins to His own account.[2]

> Blessed is the man unto whom the Lord imputeth [reckons] not iniquity.

The Passover was to be kept by Israel as a memorial of their redemption. Israel has not had a paschal lamb for almost 1900 years, since the destruction of the Temple in Jerusalem by Titus. The rabbis use as a substitute the dry shank-bone of a lamb. According to the law, the Temple was the only place for the sacrifice of the lamb. The Jewish Passover now being observed every year is without a lamb, which is a striking fulfilment of Hosea's prophecy declaring that for many days Israel is to be "without a sacrifice."

The lamb was kept for observation from the tenth to the fourteenth day of the month. No spot or blemish was to be found. The lamb must be killed and the blood shed, without a bone being broken. A living lamb could not prevent the death-angel's coming at midnight. The wonderful, holy,

1. 1 Pet. 1:20; Rev. 13:8; Eph. 1:4; Ex. 12:1-28; John 1:29; 19:36; 1 Cor. 5:6,7; Matt. 26:28; Col. 1:20; Rom. 3:24,25; 1 Pet. 1:18,19; Rev. 1:5; Lev. 17:11; Luke 23:4; 1 Pet. 1:19; Gen. 9:4
2. Ex. 13:1,2,13; 2 Cor. 5:21; Ex. 12:25-27; Luke 22:19,20; Psa. 32:1,2; Heb. 8:4,5; 10:1-3; Hosea 3:4,5

spotless earthly life of Christ could not suffice to cleanse from sin. No spot or blemish was found in Christ. His enemies had to say, We "find no fault in this man." The lamb was the basis of Israel's blessings and security, pointing to Christ:

> Ye were redeemed with the precious blood of Christ, as of a lamb without blemish and without spot.

Blood is life. "The life thereof which is the blood thereof." Christ forfeited His life for man's with His blood, which was His life.

> Through Him to reconcile all things unto Himself, having made peace through the blood of His Cross.

The substitutionary blood-atonement of Christ runs throughout the system of types in the Old Testament.

> It is the blood that maketh an atonement for the soul.

In Genesis we find God's provision for sin in the skin of the lamb:

> Unto Adam also and to his wife did the Lord God make coats of skins, and clothed them.

The skin of the sacrifice, typically, clothed the sinner. God took away the coverings of fig leaves from Adam and Eve, clothing them with coats of skins, testifying to their shame and need of covering (atonement). Adam's clothing was a badge of his sin and fall from innocency. So it is today. Both nature and man suffered from the fall. The homemade garments of leaves made by Eve would quickly wither. There must be a substitute. Only by life can life be redeemed. Here God instituted the type of the great Substitute to come. It was the first time Adam and Eve witnessed the shedding of blood and death. How terrified they must have been!

In the sacrifice of the animal, Christ is seen taking the guilt of the first Adam and his posterity. Here the gospel of grace is being preached, in type—the Lamb of God slain from the foundation of the world. The robe of His righteousness is being provided for every sinner accepting it. He is the only One able to cover sin and shame. Man has always proved a failure under license and under law because of the weakness of the human flesh. Neither can culture, environment, good works, nor heredity suffice. They do not reach and cleanse the guilty heart. The Old Testament way of coming to Christ was by sacrifice.

"The law is become our tutor to bring us unto Christ," but the law was impotent in that it could not save. Daniel turned his face toward Jerusalem, the place of sacrifice, and not toward Sinai, where the law was given.

Christ's provision for sin is also seen in Abel, who brought the firstling of his flock in sacrifice:

The Lord had respect unto Abel and to his offering:
But unto Cain and to his offering He had not respect.

The difference was not in the two brothers, but in their offerings and faith. Abel recognized himself a sinner, needing a sacrificial offering for cleansing, whereas Cain brought the works of his hands, not recognizing the necessity of a sin-offering. His was a bloodless religion. Like the Pharisee, he desired praise for his own goodness without the substitution of a blood-offering. Cain was a materialist. He could not afford to slay a lamb, but had no compunction in murdering his own brother. Cain is a type of the self-righteous natural man. He depended upon the first-fruits of the ground that God had cursed.

The true and false concepts of eternal salvation are found within these two sacrifices. Abel is a type of Christ in that Abel died on account of his brother's sin. Cain's hatred of his brother also foreshadows the Jews' rejection of their brother in the flesh, Christ, whom they delivered for death.[3]

The Old Testament word "atonement" means "to cover." The blood of the Old Testament sacrifices covered, typically, the sins of the believer, looking forward to the sacrifice of Christ as the Paschal Lamb. In the proclamation of John the Baptist, the forerunner of Christ, he says: "Behold the Lamb of God, which taketh away [or, lifts up and carries away] the sin of the world." No other Person hung on the Cross but the divine Lamb of God. None but an infinite Being could have paid the penalty for sin. Righteous judgment demands infinite suffering, hence an Infinite Sufferer. "It was the infinite Lawmaker who took the place of the lawbreaker." He who denounced the curse hangs upon the Cross as the Lamb of God to remove it.

The ass in Exodus is typical of the sinner who must be redeemed by the death of the Lamb of God:[4]

> And every firstling of an ass thou shalt redeem with a lamb; and if thou wilt not redeem it, then thou shalt break his neck: and all the first-born of man among thy children shalt thou redeem.

There is also a double-type in the record of Isaac, where the promised heir is to be offered, and the ram is provided as a substitute. Abraham says to Isaac; "My son, God will provide Himself a lamb." This He did in the substitute of a ram, a type of Christ on the Cross.[5] As the offering was carried "without the camp," so was Christ carried without the gate to Calvary and there crucified.

Again, Rahab's scarlet cord is a beautiful type of the blood of Christ, shed for the sinner. As faith in the Word

3. Gen. 3:15,21; 4:4; Luke 4:28; Heb. 2:14; 11:4; 1 John 1:7; Gal. 3:24; Jude 11
4. Ex. 29:36; 13:13; 34:20; Isa. 1:3; Lev. 9:2,3; Matt. 20:5
5. Gen. 22:8; Heb. 10:5-10; 11:17-19; Rom. 8:32; Phil. 2:5-8; Lev. 4:21; Heb. 13:11; Isa. 53:7

was salvation to Rahab, the harlot, so it is today for every believer.

> By faith the harlot Rahab perished not with them that believed not.

During all the future the Paschal Lamb will be the Light of heaven and earth, for the "Lamb is the Light thereof." [6]

Adam, Abraham, Israel, saints, and all the world have had the same gospel—salvation by sacrifice. With the children of Israel in the Old Testament, salvation came by faith, with obedience as its test. The same is true today. Christ is seen in the Bible as the center of all history, showing God's design and purpose in Him. [7]

After the suffering comes the glory. Christ's suffering as the Lamb of God could only be finished on Calvary, where He wore the crown of thorns. His glory will be manifested when He wears the crown of diadems.

Peter records how Christ "bare our sins in His own body on the tree, that we, being dead to sins, should live unto righteousness: by whose stripes ye were healed." Peter was but echoing the prophecy of Isaiah:

> He was wounded for our transgressions, He was bruised for our iniquities: the chastisement of our peace was upon Him: and with His stripes we are healed.

Here Christ is shown in His marvelous grace of substitution, that "God might be just, and the justifier of him which believeth in Jesus." In His voluntary atonement the awful problem of sin was met. Hence, in that coming Day the saints can sing that redemptive song:

> Thou art worthy . . . because thou wast slain, and hath redeemed us to God by the blood out of every kindred, and tongue, and people, and nation.

6. Joshua 2:21; Heb. 11:31; Ex. 12:13; Job 30:11; Eccl. 4:12; Hosea 11:4; Rev. 21:23

7. Isa. 50:6; 63:7-9; 53:12; 40:11; Heb. 1:9; Psa. 23; Isa. 11:3-5; Isa. 42:3; Psa. 75:2

Christ is also shown to be the compassionate One in the Old Testament:

As Substitute,	He voluntarily suffered.
As Redeemer,	He loved and pitied.
As Saviour,	He was numbered with the transgressors.
As Holy One,	He died for our sins.
As Shepherd,	He feeds His sheep.
As Judge,	He judges the meek and the poor.
As Bruised Reed,	He will not break.

Jeremiah prophesied a New Covenant whereby the Lamb was to abolish the Old: [8]

Behold, the days come, saith the Lord, that I will make a new covenant with the house of Israel, and with the house of Judah: I will put my law in their inward parts, and write it in their hearts . . . for I will forgive their iniquity, and I will remember their sin no more.

8. Jer. 31:31-34; Matt. 26:26,27; Mark 14:22-25; Luke 22:14-23

Chapter 8

CHRIST
and the Offerings

LEVITICUS IS THE BOOK OF WORSHIP, written for the redeemed. No other book in the Bible contains so many words of Jehovah: "Jehovah spake" (36 times), "I AM Jehovah" (21 times), and "I AM Jehovah your God" (21 times). The Holy Spirit is not mentioned in Leviticus as all of the types refer to Christ. The Spirit's work is to exalt and magnify the Christ. The threefold teachings of the Levitical law and offerings might be summed up in three words: Sacrifice, Separation, Satisfaction. Christ would have it so today.

The Offerings show forth, in type, the one great offering of the person of the Lord Jesus Christ, and the measure of the appreciation of Christ. There are some twenty Hebrew words in the Old Testament which are translated "offer" or "offerings." An offering could be offered for the priest, for the nation, for a ruler, or for an individual.

One of the Levitical offerings was that of a dove; typifying beauty, patience, and gentleness. The Hebrew thoroughly understood that the dove was a sacrifice for sin. No man was so poor but that he could bring such as his sin-offering. When Mary brought the babe Jesus to the Temple, her offering was a dove. At the baptism of Jesus, the Spirit came upon Him as a dove. While the dove is a type of weakness, yet the Spirit of God in the form of a dove is an emblem of power.

There are five offerings listed in Leviticus: burnt, meal, peace, sin, and trespass, all of which are typical of the person and work of Christ. The subject of these offerings is "Jesus, and Him crucified." If rightly understood, these types will correct erroneous views of sin, holiness, sanctification, salvation, and preservation.

The *burnt-offering* (Hebrew, *O lah*). This is the first of the five offerings. It represents the believer's acceptance of the person of Christ. It is also a type of Christ's life, death, and work in justification. In this offering the perfect service of Christ to God is expressed. God is satisfied with this perfect offering.

The order of the offerings is from the Godward viewpoint. They could be a bullock, sheep, he-goat, dove, or young pigeon; burned on the brazen altar and wholly consumed. The shedding of blood was absolutely necessary. Here God views the believer in Christ as justified, and perfect provision made for the sinner's guilt. Christ gave His all on the altar of sacrifice. The offerer gets nothing.

As the ashes were placed at the east end of the altar and deposited in a "clean place," so the crucified body of Jesus was placed in the clean tomb of Joseph which had never known defilement.

Isaac was a burnt-offering, typical of how Christ was to offer "Himself without spot to God."

God was in Christ reconciling the world unto Himself.

The burnt-offering speaks of justification and makes no mention of sin, for "by Him all that believe are justified from all things." The offering was "baked," a type of the sufferings of Christ, "tried as by fire." [1]

The *meal-offering* (Hebrew, *Minchah*). This offering,

1. Gen. 8:20; Lev. 1:3-17; 6:8-13; Eph. 2:1-6; Heb. 10:7; 2 Cor. 5:19; Ezra 3:2; Psa. 51:19; Acts 13:39

generally without blood, is a gift offering to secure favor. It is made of flour, frankincense, oil, and salt; typifying the life of Christ, presenting to God an unblemished manhood. The fine flour is a symbol of the perfect, sinless, and spotless life of Christ. They fed on "the bread of God." Flour is to wheat what blood is to the body, and shows that the believer should feed on the "Bread of Life." Christ is the Sustainer of life, as was, typically, the bread on the table in the holy place.[2]

The *peace-offering* (Hebrew, *Shelem*). This offering consists of a male or female of the herd or flock. Here we have "peace" on the ground of the perfection, or compensation of Christ, who, through His death, becomes our peace and reconciliation. This brings to the believer communion, fellowship, and peace with God.

The priest's portion was the "heave-shoulder" (strength) and the "wave-breast" (affection). As "priests unto God" the believer partakes of the "shoulder" for strength, and the "breast" for affection and love. This offering is one of thanksgiving by which Christ is expressing praise, communion, and fellowship with God.[3]

The *sin-* and *trespass-offerings* (Hebrew, *Chattath*).

These two offerings are the same, except in type. The sin-offering shows how Christ atoned for the sinful nature—"He was made sin for us." Sin here means "missing the mark," coming short of the requirement, or the sin of commission. This offering differs from the others in that the animal was not to be burned on the brazen altar, but "without the camp." So was the Lamb of God offered "without the camp."

Also, the blood "ran down and outward" from the offering. So with Christ on the Cross. As God hid His face

2. Lev. 2; 6:14-23; 21:17; Heb. 7:26
3. Lev. 3:1-17; 7:11-13; Rom. 5:1; Col. 1:20; Isa. 40:11; Deut. 33

from the Sin-offering, Christ cried, "My God, My God, why hast Thou forsaken me?" Sin is met in the sin-offering of Christ. The sinner is cleansed by faith in the blood (sin-offering) and not by the earthly life of Christ (meal-offering). The altar designated by God for the offering up of Christ was the "tree of the cross." He was to be made a curse for the sinner—"Cursed is every one that hangeth on a tree." Christ had to suffer the death of a bondslave. Had He died any other way, He would not have been a Sin-offering.

The trespass-offering shows Christ as the perfect Reconciler between God and man, and answerable for the sins against God and man. It speaks of Christ as bearing the believer's sinful acts and trespasses. Here the sinner's trespasses are forgiven in the One who bare them in His own body on the tree; here is the removal of sin and pardon of its guilt.

The trespass-offering comes before the *thank-offering*. One must pass through the veil of the Christ-flesh before entering the holy of holies.[4]

The offerings as found in Isaiah 53 might be classified thus:

Verse 11: By His knowledge shall My righteous servant justify many.
> Burnt-offering: Christ, the perfect Justifier.

Verse 3: He is despised and rejected of men.
> Meal-offering: Christ, the perfect Redeemer.

Verse 5: The chastisement of our peace was upon Him.
> Peace-offering: Christ, the perfect Peace.

Verse 6: The Lord hath laid on Him the iniquity of us all.
> Sin-offering: Christ, the perfect Sin-bearer.[5]

4. Lev. 4; 5; 6:1-7; Col. 2:13,14; 1 Pet. 2:24; Heb. 13:11; 2 Cor. 5:19
5. Psa. 40:6-8; Heb. 10:12,14; Isa. 53

The *red heifer-offering* differs from the five offerings of Leviticus, which are all males. They were sin-offerings for atonement and salvation. The guilt of the sinner was met at the Cross. The sins of the saint had to be confessed and forgiven at the Throne. Hence, the red heifer-offering was not for eternal salvation, but for cleansing from the daily defilement of the believer.

> And the Lord spake unto Moses and unto Aaron, saying, This is the ordinance of the law which the Lord hath commanded, saying, Speak unto the children of Israel, that they bring thee a red heifer without spot, wherein is no blemish, and upon which never came yoke . . . bring her forth without the camp, and one shall slay her before his face.

"Bring thee a red heifer," a female. "Bring her forth without the camp." Not into Egypt (type of the sinful world) but into the wilderness. Here Israel is a type of the defeated, compromising Christian, wilderness-wanderer. The red heifer (female) suggests blood and sacrificial service.

> Slay . . . and sprinkle of her blood directly before the tabernacle . . . seven times.

The blood was not to be taken into the holy of holies and placed on the mercy-seat for salvation, but was sprinkled outside before the congregation. This was a type of the daily sins of the believer, being confessed and cleansed by the once shed blood of Christ.[6]

6. Num. 19:1-4; Heb. 9:13,14; John 13

Chapter 9

CHRIST,
Calvary, and Resurrection

THE ROOTS OF THE DOCTRINES OF THE Death and Resurrection of Christ can easily be traced in type in the Old Testament. Calvary casts its shadow back over the entire Old Testament. Salvation of those ancient saints was just as certain as those of the New Testament days. Christ's triumph over sin and death at the Cross was God's plan of redemption for all people.

The Resurrection is the crowning event in the earthly life of Christ. All miracles of the Bible are established by that of the Resurrection. Deny it and all others become void. Christ was raised to an endless, supernatural life, never to die again. It was a spiritual necessity. Justice demanded it. Death had no power over Him. All spiritual blessings come through the death and Resurrection of Christ. He "died for our sins according to the scriptures." He "was raised again for our justification."

Christianity is built upon belief in the actual bodily resurrection of the Lord. The idea of the Resurrection has been removed from the realm of conjecture into the realm of fact. Most of Paul's reasoning and arguments were based on the Old Testament Scriptures. In his exhortation to Timothy he said: "From a child thou hast known the holy scriptures." Again the apostle Paul stated his gospel:

> How that Christ died for our sins according to the scriptures; And that He was buried, and that He rose again the third day according to the scriptures.

Paul affirms the Resurrection as an indisputable fact. This was the gospel of the death, burial, and resurrection of Christ according to the Old Testament Scriptures, as the New Testament had not then been written. The same thought is expressed by Luke's quoting Christ after His Resurrection:

> And He said unto them, These are the words which I spake unto you, while I was yet with you, that all things must be fulfilled, which were written in the law of Moses, and in the prophets, and in the psalms, concerning Me. Then opened He their understanding, that they might understand the scriptures, and said unto them, Thus it is written, and thus it behooved Christ to suffer, and to rise from the dead the third day.

Death and resurrection are foreshadowed in nature, beginning with the first chapter in Genesis:

> And the earth brought forth grass, and herb yielding seed after its kind, and the tree yielding fruit, whose seed was in itself, after his kind; and God saw that it was good.

Here we have the seed dying and buried in the earth with its life germ, bringing forth grass, herb, and fruit upon the earth. The germ-seed in death craves life from above. The aim of every organic thing is propagation-life, not self-preservation. We have here the introduction of life, organic matter created out of inorganic matter, death. The grain dies as a grain and reappears as a stalk. The believer-man dies as a son of Adam, and is resurrected as a glorified son of God. This was on the "third day" of creation, the number of resurrection. "And the evening and the morning were the third day." There was the setting sun, evening, darkness—Death. There was the morning, light—Resurrection. There was fall and winter—Death. There was spring and summer—resurrection.

> Except a corn of wheat fall into the ground and die, it abideth alone: but if it die, it bringeth forth much fruit.

Paul said, "To die is gain."

The creation of the heavenly bodies, the sun, moon, stars, tell of Death and Resurrection:

> And God made two great lights; the greater light to rule by day, and the lesser light to rule the night; He made the stars also.

Paul added:

> There is one glory of the sun, and another glory of the moon, and another glory of the stars: for one star differeth from another star in glory. So also the resurrection of the dead. It is sown in corruption [death]; it is raised in incorruption [life].

The Lord caused a deep sleep (death) to fall upon Adam, and opened his flesh, taking a bone, and brought forth life, Eve. Adam was also raised from this deep sleep of death, a figure of Christ who was to come. Paul said:

> Nevertheless death reigned from Adam to Moses, even over them that had not sinned after the similitude of Adam's transgression, who is the figure of Him that was to come.

Adam's body was wounded: so was Christ's. Adam brought forth a bride from his wounded side; so will Christ. Adam was raised from his "deep sleep"; so was Christ. From the pierced side of Christ came life, resurrection, and immortality.

For Adam and Eve "The Lord God made coats of skins, and clothed them." This slain animal (probably a lamb) was the first offering for the Atonement (covering). Here in substitution is the first step toward the Cross. Grace enters and is manifested as soon as sin is seen. Adam lost his fellowship and communion with his Maker. Now we see the first gospel message of substitution, the innocent dying for the guilty. Here the death of Christ is foreshadowed, showing God's marvelous grace.

Only man necessitates an artificial covering. Creatures of the earth and air have their proper coverings naturally developed from within. In sin man lost his natural raiment of light. In the death-sin of man, God provides Calvary for man's salvation. The sinner becomes clothed in His righteousness.

In Abel's day we have the offering of Cain and Abel: "The Lord had respect unto Abel and to his offering." It pointed to Calvary. Cain would reject the substitutionary work of the Cross, bringing his ethical, cultural, and self-righteous endeavors as a propitiation.

In Abraham's day God promised Sarah a son, but "It ceased to be with Sarah after the manner of women." Sarah at eighty had passed the age of human propagation. Abraham laughed when the promise of a son was given. "But God," faithful to His promise, brought life from the dead womb of the woman; pointing, in type, to the Death and Resurrection of Christ.

In the offering of Isaac we have a double type of the Death and Resurrection of Christ. Isaac was offered up and the ram was provided as a substitute. Abraham said to the two young men, "on the third day [number of resurrection] I and the lad will go yonder and worship, and *come* again to you." Abraham had faith, to believe that if Isaac died God was able to raise him again. This is another beautiful type of the Death and Resurrection of Christ, and is verified in the Epistle to the Hebrews:

Accounting that God was able to raise him [Isaac] up, even from the dead; from whence also he received him in a figure.

Mount Moriah where Isaac was offered means "The mountain of provision." Here, in type, was the provision of the Lamb of God which should take away the sin of the world. This clearly speaks of the Messiah in the person of Isaac, ready and willing to be offered as a sacrifice upon the altar.

In Moses' day, regarding the Passover Lamb, God said: "When I see the blood, I will pass over you." This is another type of Calvary, where the Passover-Lamb was to die for the sins of the world. Those behind the blood were saved and safe. As a type of redemption we read;

> And every firstling of an ass thou shalt redeem with a lamb; and if thou wilt not redeem it, then thou shalt break his neck: and all the first-born of man among thy children shalt thou redeem.

The first-born must be redeemed by the death of a lamb. This beautiful type was exemplified in the death of the anti-type, Christ, the Lamb of God.

When Israel was famishing for water in the wilderness, we find that the bitter waters of Marah were sweetened by a "tree" cast into the waters. Here is a type of the Cross, making sweet the assurance of a perfect cleansing in Christ, the "water of life" to the thirsty soul.

God said to Moses, "Thou shalt smite the rock, and there shall come water out of it." Paul says, "That Rock was Christ." Moses was kept from Canaan because he smote the rock the second time instead of "speaking" to it. Christ need be smitten but once for sin.

God instructed Moses that no malefactor was to hang all night upon a tree, saying, "His body shall not remain all night upon the tree . . . (for he that is hanged is accursed of God)." Paul wrote: "Christ hath redeemed us from the curse of the law, being made a curse for us: for it is written, Cursed is every one that hangeth on a tree."

Israel had sinned and rebelled against Jehovah. Fiery serpents were sent whose bite meant death. After Moses had prayed, Jehovah instructed him to set up the image of a fiery serpent and the people looking upon the uplifted serpent would be healed. This again pointed to Christ uplifted upon the Cross of Calvary, as Jesus intimated to Nicodemus.

In the days of the priests they were to carry forth the bullock "without the camp and burn him." Christ was carried "without the camp" to be crucified, becoming the sin-offering for the believer.

In the Levitical offering for leprosy, the clean, *dead* bird (killed in an earthen vessel) was a type of Christ on Calvary, a clean sacrifice without blemish. The clean, *live* bird, was to dip its wings in the blood of the dead bird, and then loosed for the air; a beautiful type of Christ in death, resurrection, and ascension.

In Aaron's day the seed buried in the ground brought forth harvest and the first-fruits, the sheaf of which was waved by the priest before the Lord on the day *after* the Sabbath (Sunday). Sunday is the first day, typifying resurrection. Hence, we have in the buried seed, death; and in the first-fruits, resurrection.

When God was seeking a High Priest, "The rod of Aaron . . . budded, and brought forth buds, and bloomed blossoms, and yielded almonds." Aaron's rod was dead, as were the other rods of the twelve tribes. His alone before the Lord became alive, and Aaron became the high priest. Here is a type of Christ in death and resurrection, becoming the high priest after the order of Melchisedec.

In Joshua's day, Rahab the harlot, "bound the *scarlet* line in the window," thus saving herself and her household. "By faith the harlot Rahab perished not with them that believed not." Here was faith in action, and salvation by the scarlet cord, typifying Christ on Calvary. Rahab's faith is shown in her covenant with the spies, and her faithfulness to that covenant, which saved her from physical death. Those not included in the covenant, perished.

There is a well-known ceremony still practised by the Jews in connection with their Day of Atonement. A fowl is killed, its blood being shed as an atonement for sin. In the Talmudic Hebrew the word for *fowl* is *gever*. The Hebrew name for *man* is also *gever*. The fowl, *gever*, dies as man's substitute. In Zechariah the man (Christ Jesus) is called Gever, and is Messianic.

Samson found "honey in the carcase of the lion." Samson slew the lion in order to get to his expected bride. Afterward upon returning he found "honey in the carcase." Out of the death of Christ come the blessings and sweetness of salvation. Christ upon returning to earth will have His bride in victory and glory.[1]

The prophet Isaiah declared:

> Thy dead shall live; my dead bodies shall arise. Awake and sing, ye that dwell in the dust; for thy dew is as the dew of herbs, and the earth shall cast forth the dead.

These predictions of the Old Testament saints became a reality when Christ arose from the dead.

Job asked the question, "If a man die, shall he live again?" He answered his own question by saying, "I know that my Redeemer liveth." Job was here pointing to the Death and Resurrection of Christ.

The Psalmist cried out in assurance, "Thou wilt not leave my soul in hell [sheol]; neither wilt thou suffer thine Holy One to see corruption."

Zechariah prophesied, "They shall look upon me whom they have pierced . . . smite the shepherd, and the sheep

1. Deut. 21:23; Gal. 3:13; Num. 21:8; John 3:14,15; John 12:24; Luke 24:44; 1 Cor. 15:1-4; Gen. 1:11,12; 2:21; 3:21; 4:4; 18:11; 22:1-14; Heb. 11:19; Ex. 12:13; 13:13; 15:23-25; 17:6; Lev. 4:21; 14:5,6,50-53; 23:7-13; Num. 17:8; Joshua 2:21; Judges 14:8; Psa. 16:10; Rom. 5:14; 6:9,10

shall be scattered." One of the Roman soldiers pierced His side, minutely fulfilling this prophecy.

Daniel prophesying the resurrection said:

> And many of them that sleep in the dust of the earth shall awake, some to everlasting life, and some to shame and everlasting contempt.

The expression "born" or "begotten" refers to the three-fold manifestation of Christ: His pre-existent state, "the first-born of all creation"; His birth of Mary, "There is born to you"; and His Resurrection, "The first-born from the dead."

A threefold picture of the resurrection is seen:

in word, "For I know that my Redeemer liveth, and that He shall stand at the latter day upon the earth."

in figure, "From whence also he received him [Isaac] in a figure." Isaac was a ready offering, raised from the Altar.

in prophecy, "Thy dead shall live: my dead bodies shall arise."

This is a glorious promise of the resurrection of the children of God.[2]

2. Isa. 26:19; Job 14:14; 19:25-27; Zech. 12:10; 13:7; John 19:34; Heb. 11:19; Gen. 22:1-14; Dan. 12:2; Col. 1:15,18; Rev: 1:5; Luke 2:11; Deut. 27:26; Gal. 3:10 RV

Chapter 10

CHRIST
Prophet—Priest—King

THESE THREEFOLD PROPHECIES ARE found in the Old Testament:

I will raise them up a Prophet.
I will raise Me up a faithful Priest.
I will raise unto David a righteous Branch, and a King.

The prophets, priests, and kings of Israel were anointed and divinely ordained. As Prophet, Christ was God's representative and spokesman, revealing His will, mind, and heart to man. As Priest, He is revealed as Mediator between God and man, interceding and pleading the interests of His people. As King, He will reign over men, enforcing the laws of God. Christ is not now reigning on the earth as King except in the hearts of believers. He has not yet received the kingdom. He taught His disciples to pray "Thy kingdom come." He is now the Head of the church.

CHRIST THE PROPHET

The Hebrew word for prophet is *navi* from the root *nava* meaning to "boil up, boil forth"—to pour forth words from a higher power than their own—one who forthtells and foretells, or "speaks forth" the Word of Jehovah, relative to present and future events.

The test of a true prophet is found in the words of Jehovah in Deuteronomy:

I will raise them up a prophet from among their
brethren . . . and will put My words in his mouth;
and he shall speak unto them all that I shall command.
When a prophet speaketh in the name of the Lord, if
the thing follow not, nor come to pass, that is the
thing which the Lord hath not spoken, but the prophet
hath spoken it presumptuously: thou shalt not be afraid
of him.

Moses is regarded as the first and greatest of the Hebrew
prophets. The "Law" and the "Prophets" are two great
divisions of the Old Testament. The Law consists of the
five books of Moses (the Pentateuch) while the Prophets
comprise the major and minor prophets.

Christ was the true Prophet. He bade men heed the Law
of Moses and the words of the prophets, saying: "Think not
that I am come to destroy the law, or the prophets; I am not
come to destroy, but to fulfill."

The prophet receives the message, speaks, communicates it
to men. Christ, as Prophet, received the message of God and
in this spirit did His work. A prophet works as well as
speaks. So Christ, as the Word-Prophet (*Logos*) acted
throughout the Old Testament dispensation. He is the one
that comes from God to man, with a message, to live, suffer,
and die. The suffering-prophet of the Psalmist is a type of
the awful suffering of the Christ-Prophet:

I sink in deep mire, where there is no standing:
I am come into deep waters, where the floods overflow me. I am weary of my crying: my throat is dried;
mine eyes fail while I wait for my God. They that hate
me without a cause are more than the hairs of mine
head: they that would destroy me, being mine enemies
wrongfully.

It was the Christ-Prophet who was to come and die as a
Substitute, the Son of man, and the Son of God. The twenty-
second Psalm is called the "Psalm of Sobs." It describes the

sufferings on Calvary. Here for six hours the Jesus-Prophet hung, a spectacle to men and demons. No wonder Jeremiah exclaimed:

> Is it nothing to you, all ye that pass by? Behold, and see if there be any sorrow like unto my sorrow, which is done unto me, wherewith the Lord hath afflicted me in the day of His fierce anger.

The dying Prophet satisfied the judgment of a righteous God, typically, at the brass altar of the Tabernacle in the wilderness; bringing salvation, sanctification, and preservation to the believer. He was the One sent to represent the King, with a message to an alien country, until called from a Prophet to Priesthood. Christ is the Prophet by His manifestation in incarnation—God manifest in the flesh. He was a Priest by resurrection and intercession. He is King in coming glory.

The believer should beware of false prophets in these latter days:

> But there were false prophets also among the people, even as there shall be false teachers among you, who privily shall bring in damnable heresies, even denying the Lord that bought them, and bring upon themselves swift destruction.

The Old Testament prophets were spiritual guides to their own day as well as revealers of what the future contained.[1]

CHRIST THE PRIEST

A priest has been defined as "a public person who deals with an offended God in the name of the guilty, for reconciliation, by sacrifice, which he offered to God upon an altar, being thereto called of God, that he may be accepted."

1. Deut. 18:15-18,22; 1 Sam. 2:35; Jer. 23:5; Rev. 19:13; John 1:3-14; Col. 1:17,18; 1 Pet. 1:10-12; Psa. 69:2; Isa. 53:6; 2 Cor. 5:21; 1 Pet. 2:4; John 3:16; 10:17,18; Ex. 27:1-6; Num. 21:8,9; Rev. 1:15; 2 Pet. 2:1; Num. 6:24-26

A priest becomes the medium of access to God in relation to a sacrifice and sinners needing reconciliation.

The words "priest" and "priesthood" occur 165 times in Leviticus, the book of the priesthood. There are no earthly priests at present upon the earth. The priesthood was from the tribe of Levi. Jesus was of the tribe of Judah, hence could not have been an earthly priest. The believers' access to God is not through an earthly priest, but through Christ, the heavenly High Priest, now at the right hand of the Father. Such a Priest must be holy, harmless, undefiled, sinless, and incapable of sinning.[2]

The words "holy" and "holiness" occur 101 times in Leviticus, having reference to the believers' approach to God through the Christ-Priest. Aaron is a type of Christ, and entered the most holy place with blood from the altar of sacrifice on the day of the atonement. So did Christ with the shedding of His blood enter the holy of holies in behalf of the sinner. Some day the believer will hear from the most holy place the threefold Aaronic benediction:

> The Lord bless thee and keep thee: The Lord make His face to shine upon thee, and be gracious unto thee: The Lord lift up His countenance upon thee and give thee peace.

The Apostle Paul, in showing the priesthood of Christ to be superior to that of Aaron, cites Melchisedec who is described in Genesis as "priest of the most high God" with no genealogy, beginning, or ending but "made like unto the Son of God," thus making him a perfect type of Christ in His character of heavenly Priest, and in his name which means "King of Righteousness," "the Lord our Righteousness," "King of Peace," a name which only could be ap-

2. 1 Sam. 2:35; Heb. 5:4; 7:26; Gen. 14:18-20; Isa. 11:4-9; John 17; Job 9:33; 1 Pet. 2:5; Lev. 8:1-6; Rom. 12:1; Eph. 5:25; Heb. 1:9; 4:8; 5:10; Lev. 9:10; Hosea 11:1; Isa. 46:9,10

plied to the Christ-Priest. Paul concludes his argument by saying:

> And without all contradiction the less is blessed of the better. And here men that die receive tithes; but there he receiveth them, of whom it is witnessed *that He liveth.* So also Christ glorified not Himself to be made an high-priest; but He that said unto Him, Thou art My Son, today have I begotten Thee. As he saith also in another place, Thou art a priest forever after the order of Melchisedec.

While Christ is the High Priest after the order of Melchisedec, yet His work is also patterned after that of Aaron. The priest is one who goes from man to God, and intercedes for the people. Christ is the High Priest, Mediator, and Intercessor between God and man. Believers are to be "kings and priests unto God," and are of the "holy priesthood, . . . acceptable to God by Jesus Christ."

The law of the priesthood found in Leviticus is that of *consecration.* The priests could not consecrate themselves.[3] Someone has aptly said of the priests:

> *Presentation,* they had to present their bodies.
> *Dedication,* the anointing oil was only for the priests.
> *Application,* the blood was applied on the ear and hand.
> *Separation,* the food was separated and consecrated.
> *Ministration,* the ministry of the offerings were before
>   the Lord.

The Old Testament priesthood was not continued after the control of the Roman Empire. The high office had fallen into corruption before the coming of Christ.

Joshua was a type of Christ, in the prophetic office; Melchisedec in the priesthood; and David in the office of kingship.

---

3. John 10:11; Heb. 13:21; 4:14-16; 1 Pet. 5:4; Acts 1:9-11; 1 John 2:1-2; Acts 5:31; John 16:7,8; Mark 16:19,20; Deut. 18:15-22; Mark 13:22; 2 Pet. 2:1

The emerald was in the breastplate of the high priest, representing praise and adoration. The breastplate with its brilliant stones, each bearing the name of one of the tribes of Israel, was worn close to the breast of the priest. This is a beautiful type of Christ, our High Priest, taking the believer close to His loving heart.

CHRIST THE KING

"I will raise up unto David a righteous Branch . . . a King." Whenever the blessings to the nation of Israel are mentioned in the Old Testament they are connected with the coming of the "King of the Jews." Therefore, when the Old Testament closed, many prophecies relative to the King of Israel were still unfulfilled.

Zechariah was sent with a message of the coming of the King:

> Rejoice greatly, O daughter of Zion; shout, O daughter of Jerusalem: behold, thy King cometh unto thee: He is just, and having salvation; lowly, and riding upon an ass.

This prophecy was fulfilled when Jesus came to cleanse the temple and to present Himself as King of the Jews; but He was rejected. When He comes the second time (as a result of Zechariah 12:10) Israel will say, "Blessed is He that cometh in the name of the Lord." Pilate said, "Behold your King," and a superscription was written, "This is Jesus the King of the Jews."

The Gospel of Matthew pictures Christ as King of the Jews, with the legal right to the Davidic throne. This right is established in His genealogy. He was the last Jew to establish such a claim.

The "kingdom of heaven" is mentioned 32 times in Matthew, and nowhere else in the New Testament.

The acts of the gracious and thoughtful King-Christ are described as:

The King's wrath is as the roaring of a lion; but his favor is as dew upon the grass.

The proclamation of His coming is as, "Wonderful, Counsellor, The Mighty God, The Everlasting Father, The Prince of Peace." The King was announced to Mary as "the Son of the Highest" and was sought by the wise men, saying, "Where is He that is born King of the Jews?"

Christ is referred to as the reigning King, who is to have the nations and heathen as an inheritance, as when the psalmist wrote:

Kiss the Son, lest He be angry . . . when His wrath is kindled but a little. Blessed are all they that put their trust in Him.

Only eternity will be sufficient to reveal the full beauty of the JEHOVAH-KING when we shall see Him face to face:

Thine eyes shall see the King in His beauty.
Seek the Lord and His strength, seek His face continually.[4]

The psalmist sang,

Who is the King of glory? Jehovah strong and mighty, Jehovah mighty in battle.

Isaiah in vision said,

I saw the Lord sitting upon a throne, high and lifted up . . . for mine eyes have seen the King, Jehovah of Hosts.

Jeremiah exclaimed,

The King, whose name is Jehovah of hosts.

4. Jer. 23:5; Zech. 9:9; Matt. 21:1-9; John 1:11; 19:14-19; Zech. 12:10; Matt. 23:39; 27:37; Mark 15:26; Luke 23:38; 1:30-33; Prov. 19:12; Isa. 9:6; Matt. 2:1,2; Psa. 2:12; Isa. 33:17; 1 Chron. 16:11; 2 Cor. 3:18

Joel in prophecy referred to the coming King in Judgment, saying,

> Let the heathen . . . come up to the valley of Jehoshaphat: for there will I sit to judge all.

And Matthew added,

> He shall sit upon the throne of His glory.

The last book of the Old Testament refers to the King of judgment:

> For I am a great King, saith the Lord of hosts, and My name is dreadful among the heathen.

In the threefold Messianic psalms (22,23,24) we have:

Christ, as Prophet, on the Cross; "hath appeared," past;
Christ, as Priest, on the Throne; "now appears," present;
Christ, as King, at His coming; "shall appear," future.

As Prophet, saving from the penalty of sin at the Cross;
As Priest, saving from the power of sin at the throne;
As King, saving from the presence of sin at His coming.

Prophet, the Good Shepherd, that giveth His life for His sheep;
Priest, the Great Shepherd, that leadeth His sheep;
King, the Chief Shepherd, who shall appear with His sheep.

Prophet, Christ the Anointed, coming from God to man;
Priest, Christ the Intercessor, going from man to God;
King, Christ the Messiah-Judge, who is coming to rule.

Prophet, whose redemptive work ended at the Cross, "It is finished";
Priest, who is now appearing in glory for His own;
King, who will function as Judge when He comes to reign.[5]

5. Psa. 22; 23; 24; Heb. 9:24-28; S. of S. 2:4; 6:4; Ex. 28:33; Zech. 14:20; Psa. 55:18; Isa. 6:1-5; Jer. 46:18; 48:15; Mal. 1:14; John 10:11; 16:7,8; Heb. 13:21; 4:14-16; 1 Pet. 5:4; 1 John 2:1,2; Acts 5:31; Mark 16:19,20

As Prophet, "He appeared to put away sin," justification;

As Priest, He now appears "in the presence of God for
us," preservation;

As King, "Unto them that look for Him shall He
appear," glorification.

Prophet, in suffering and death we see Christ in humiliation;

Priest, risen at right hand of the Father, Christ in exaltation;

King, in coming glory, Christ in coronation.

Chapter 11

CHRIST
and the Feasts in Leviticus

THESE SEVEN FEASTS WERE INSTITUTED by God as annual religious festivals among the Jews to perpetuate the memory of some great event, and to keep alive the expectations regarding the coming Messiah. They were also appointed seasons when God called upon Israel to celebrate past deliverances and present blessings. These feasts were all typical of Christ and His redemptive work in various aspects. They speak of Christ in the fulfilment of God's eternal purpose for Israel and the Church.

PASSOVER FEAST (Hebrew *pasach*)

The name "Passover" is one given the Paschal lamb—the victim—slain by the Israelites, assuring the safety of the first-born in Egypt and passed over where blood was sprinkled on the doorway. The lamb was selected four days before the Passover, which is celebrated on the fourteenth day of Nisan (first month), the same time that Christians celebrate "Easter," followed by the seven days' Feast of Unleavened Bread. Jesus entered Jerusalem four days before His crucifixion.

This Feast was also called the feast of unleavened bread, and was a reminder of the past grace of God and an obligation to trust Him for future blessings. The Apostle Paul commanded to "purge out the old leaven" (a type of sin) "for even Christ our Passover is sacrificed for us." At this time the "cup of thanksgiving" was also passed and partaken of, and a song of praise for deliverance from bondage was sung.

After the destruction of Jerusalem the Jews ceased their offering of sacrifices, but still observed the Passover with only unleavened bread. It is now celebrated by the Jewish people as their New Year. The Passover marks the beginning of the religious year in counter-distinction of the *civil* year. As the feast of redemption it is the basis of the three great Jewish festivals, regulating all their other sacred institutions. Jesus often attended these Feasts, the last of which was just before His own sacrifice on the Cross.[1] This Passover feast is a constant reminder of the work to be accomplished by the true Passover Lamb on Calvary. Christ became the believers' sanctification as the Lamb upon the Cross.

FEAST OF UNLEAVENED BREAD (Hebrew *matzos*)

This was a feast of Jehovah with unleavened bread. Israel was to put away all leavened bread from their homes. Leaven is always a type of sin, to be judged in the light of Calvary.

Twelve loaves of unleavened bread were to be offered to the Lord, and then to the priests. This unleavened bread was typical of Christ as the Bread of Life, the Sustainer, as well as of communion with Him in holy living. The believers' holiness is found only in Christ. Unleavened bread is typical of Christ in redemption, and of His giving strength for the journey of life.

At the Passover the believer signified *relationship* with Christ; at the feast of unleavened bread he had *fellowship* with Him.

1. Lev. 23; Gen. 40:20; 1 Cor. 11:24-26; 5:7; 10:6; Ex. 12:12,13; 13:3-10; Isa. 31:5; Deut. 16:2,6,16; 2 Chron. 30:1,13-17; Ezra 6:22; Luke 22:1-23; Matt. 26:17-30; Mark 14:12-26; John 13

Purge out therefore the old leaven, that ye may be a new lump, as ye are unleavened. For even Christ our passover is sacrificed for us.

This was strictly a Jewish festival, and no stranger or uncircumcised person was permitted within the circle.[2]

FEAST OF THE FIRSTFRUITS

This, the first of the early harvest, was presented to God as a part of the harvest. It was an expression of thanksgiving on the second day after the Passover. It was also a revenue for the priests and Levites, who were custodians of the Tabernacle and worship. The firstfruits were brought to the Temple and waved before the Lord. Christ is the "firstfruit" in resurrection. He is the Priest that waves the sheaf on the first day—Sunday—resurrection day:

Now is Christ risen from the dead, and become the firstfruits of them that slept.

Christ was *dead* at the Passover, but *arose* at the feast of the firstfruits. He is also the forerunner of the believer in resurrection.[3]

FEAST OF PENTECOST

This was the second of the great feasts. It came fifty days after the wave sheaf, at the end of the harvest season. In the Old Testament it is called the feast of harvest, and was doubtless instituted when the law was given at Mount Sinai. Israel was compelled to keep it. This feast was to be a thanksgiving to God for the grain harvest.

The word "Pentecost" means fifty, the number of days between the resurrection of Christ and Pentecost. Christ

2. Lev. 23:6-8; 1 Cor. 15:20,23; 2 Cor. 7:1; Gal. 5:7-9
3. 2 Chron. 31:4-12; Ezek. 20:40; Neh. 10:35-37; Mal. 3:8; Lev. 23:10-14; 1 Cor. 15:20

showed Himself to His disciples for forty days after His resurrection, until a few days before Pentecost. However, the exact number of days is indicated in Leviticus, showing that Pentecost was celebrated fifty days after the offering of the "sheaf of the firstfruits." This came on the second day after the Passover, or "the morrow after the sabbath." It was on the first day of the Passover that the Lord was crucified; hence there are fifty days from the Resurrection to Pentecost.

On the day of Pentecost the Holy Spirit came upon the early church, designed to empower it during this gospel dispensation. Pentecost began this present dispensation when Christ is gathering out a people for His Name through the power of the Holy Spirit, after which He will come for His own.[4]

FEASTS OF TRUMPETS

This was a New Year festival, after the gathering of the harvest. The beginning of the year was heralded by the blowing of trumpets. The day was solemnly kept. Business was forbidden: "A sabbath, a memorial of blowing of trumpets."

Trumpets sounded on the great day of the atonement, at the year of Jubilee, in the bringing up of the ark, in the anointing of kings, and the dedication of Solomon's temple.

The sound of the trumpet will announce the Second Coming of Christ, as it was a token of Jehovah's coming on Mount Sinai. The lesson in the feast of the trumpets is the return of Christ to the earth, and the regathering of His people. This is anticipated when the last "trump" of the present age of grace shall sound, and "the dead [in Christ] shall be raised incorruptible, and we shall be changed."

4. Num. 28:26; Ex. 23:14-17; 34:22; 23:16; Acts 2:1-41; Lev. 23:15; Matt. 9:37,38; John 4:35,36; Acts 15:13-17; 1 Cor. 12:13

FEAST OF ATONEMENT

This day of expiation was observed yearly for fasting and rest, five days before the feast of tabernacles. This was a national call to repentance for Israel, to confess her guilt. On this day the high priest, dressed in a robe of white, entered the holy of holies, with a vessel filled with incense, and with blood from the brazen altar, which he sprinkled before and upon the mercy seat. This typified the covering of Israel's sins (atonement) and came after the blowing of the trumpets. This feast of the atonement pointed to Christ, whose expiation made satisfaction for sin and canceled its penalty. Christ is the Sin-Offering, the Lamb of God, who putteth away sin by the sacrifice of Himself. On the day of atonement we find Christ revealing Himself to Israel, and also as Sin-Bearer to the heavy-laden sinner of today.

FEAST OF TABERNACLES

This name comes from the booths in which the Israelites dwelt during the feast. They were made of trees, branches, leaves, etc. At this feast the men were required to gather once a year at Jerusalem. The festival commemorated the forty years' wanderings of Israel in the wilderness, and was also a season of thanksgiving for the harvest, called the feast of ingatherings. This was one of the three great feasts of the year, and points to the glory revealed in Christ, the Glory of the Lord. Such glory shall be shared by His saints some future day at the Second Coming of the Lord.[5]

Twice in the Gospel of John we read the "feast of the Jews." It would appear that the feasts of Jehovah had de-

5. Isa. 27:13; Matt. 24:31; Lev. 25:9; 2 Sam. 6:5; 1 Kgs. 1:34; Num. 29:1,7; Lev. 23:24; Ex. 19:16-19; Matt. 24:31; 1 Cor. 15:52; 1 Thess. 4:16; Ezek. 11:23; 43:2; Zech. 14:4,16-21; 12:10 to 13:6; Heb. 9:7; John 1:29; 1 Cor. 5:7; Eph. 1:7; Heb. 9:26; Deut. 16:13-16; Ex. 23:16; 34:22; Num. 14:21; Isa. 6:3; 40:5; Ezek. 43:2; Lev. 23:34-44; Eph. 6:12

generated into "feasts of the Jews." Such feasts had become occasions of display rather than heartfelt worship of the Lord. Should not this be a warning to the churches today in the meaningless observing of Christian ordinances?

Chapter 12

CHRIST
in Isaiah

THE PROPHET ISAIAH, THE SON OF AMOZ, prophesied in 700 B.C., during the reign of Uzziah, Jotham, Ahaz, and Hezekiah. His prophetic message was twofold: predicting the suffering and reign of Christ. We shall follow this twofold predictive life of Christ as we come to it in the prophecies of Isaiah. He described the characteristics of Christ hundreds of years before Christ was born. The truthfulness of this description is shown from quotations in the Gospel of Matthew.[1]

Isaiah 1:2-9 prophesied of the days of apostasy and declension of Judah. However, present conditions have not improved the character and conduct of man. Never was there a day when there was such a disregard for law, increase of crime, greed, selfishness, cheapness of life, and inefficiency in the courts. We have thrown to the winds the immortal words of the great American liberator, Abraham Lincoln, who said: "Let reverence of law be breathed by every American mother to her lisping babe that prattles in her lap; let it be taught in school, and in college; let it be written in primers, spelling books, and almanacs; let it be preached from the pulpit, proclaimed in legislative halls, and enforced in courts of justice."

Isaiah 1:3 foretold: "The ox knoweth its owner, and the ass his master's crib." Here we have the patient, suffering ox,

---

1. Matt. 1:21-23; Luke 2:28-35; 24:46-48; Acts 2:30-32; 15:14-16

typifying a servant of Christ, more interested in the Giver than His gift. In verse 18 the "snow" is a type of that servant in his pure, stainless, character. In that verse the gracious invitation of Christ is extended: "Come now, and let us reason together, saith Jehovah: though your sins be as scarlet, they shall be as white as snow."

In Isaiah 2:1-22 we have a picture of the last days. "The day of the Lord" (Hebrew *yom Jehovah*), a prediction of that future golden age of the Old Testament when Christ shall rule and reign on the earth. This will be characterized by the Second Coming and conquest of Christ, closing with judgments upon Satan and his followers. This is a time when wars will cease, with external peace resulting from the reign of Christ.[2]

In Isaiah 4:6 is promised "a place of refuge, and . . . a covert . . . from rain." The rain of this passage is typical of the grace of God through the suffering Christ, the Comforter of the weary follower in the journey of life. He is also the Covert of this verse, protecting those resting beneath His loving care.

Isaiah 5:26:

> And He [the Lord] will lift up an ensign to the nations from far, and will hiss unto them from the end of the earth.

Here the Lord is lifting high His ensign, a banner at the head of His victorious soldiers of the Cross. Christ will be Victor.

In Isaiah 6:3-6 the young prophet had a vision of Jehovah on His throne "high and lifted up," in majesty, sovereignty, holiness, and ascension glory; saying through the Cherubim, "Holy, holy, holy, is the Lord of hosts: the whole earth is full of His glory." The incense from the golden altar filled

2. Isa. 1:2-9; 32:1,2; 41:20; John 12:41; Micah 4:3; Jer. 23:5; Psa. 9:18; Psa. 24:6-10; Rev. 19:11-21; 20:1; Psa. 2; Isa. 22:22; Luke 15:5

the temple with smoke. The live coal from the brazen altar tells of the purifying, sanctifying power of Christ as He purges and destroys the sins of His people. Christ, as the Holy One of Israel is mentioned twenty-five times in the prophecies of Isaiah. He has the requisites of an Advocate-Priest preparing to come as King.

Isaiah 7:14:

Behold, a [the] virgin shall conceive, and bear a son, and shall call His name Immanuel [God with us].

This is a prophecy of the incarnation of Christ, and is emphasized in Isaiah 9:6 where the kingship of Christ is foretold. The "shoulder" typifies strength and power with which Christ will govern the nations in the day of His sovereign reign.

In Isaiah 11:1,5,9,10 Christ, Israel's Deliverer, is compared to a "branch" of the stem of Jesse, blending together His First and Second Advents. Christ came from His ancestor, Jesse, as the "roots" are unseen; so was Christ before Jesse. He is now the exalted "Branch." In verse five Christ is the "girdle," securing and encompassing His own dependent servants. The external peace and safety are extended to the animal world. The curse is removed and "the earth shall be full of the knowledge of Jehovah, as the waters cover the sea."

Isaiah 13:12, 4,5:

I will make a man more precious than fine gold; even a man than the golden wedge of Ophir.

Gold is a type of Deity, but the anti-type is greater than the type. Gold adorns, but Christ is more precious than gold. The gold standard may be a criterion on earth, but Christ is the perfect standard for earth and heaven.

Verse four shows that Christ will bring judgment to the

earth. It is said that there are three hundred million more heathen in the world today than when Paul finished his world-wide preaching tour. But God will see that "the earth shall be filled with the glory of the Lord."

Isaiah 14:3:

> And it shall come to pass in the day that Jehovah shall give thee rest from thy sorrow.

This is the "day" of Israel's "rest," the ushering in by the rising of the Sun of Righteousness. "Then will the Lord have mercy on Jacob." Surely this scattered and persecuted nation needs a refuge and rest!

Isaiah 21:12: "The watchman said, The morning cometh, and also the night." The Christ-Watchman, the Prophet, is here pictured as coming with a message from the Father, telling of the *morning* when His people shall be gathered to meet Him in the air, in contrast with the darkness of sin prevailing on the earth.

In the bulwarks of Isaiah 26:1,4 Christ is seen in strength and power as He protects and keeps His children. "For in the Lord Jehovah is everlasting strength," a type of Christ the "Rock of Ages." [3]

Isaiah 28:2,16-20: Christ, as Judge, is shown in these verses:

> As a tempest of hail and a destroying storm . . . and the hail shall sweep away the refuge of lies, and the waters shall overflow the hiding place.

The writer makes it plain that excuses will not suffice in the day of Judgment.

> For the bed is shorter than that a man can stretch himself on it: and the covering narrower than that he can wrap himself in it.

3. Isa. 17:9; Jer. 23:5; Zech. 3:8; Num. 14:21; 1 Thess. 4:16-18; 2 Tim. 1:12; 1 Pet. 1:5

Christ is seen in verse sixteen as the "foundation stone, a tried stone, a precious corner stone, a sure foundation." He is the stay and security of His believing ones that are in the center of God's will.

In Isaiah 29:5 Christ is manifested in judgment. He likens His enemies to "small dust . . . and . . . as chaff that passeth away," whom He shall punish at the last day. The same thought is expressed where He reveals the terrible destruction awaiting the sinner, where "the breath of the Lord [is] like a stream of brimstone." While such passages primarily apply to the judgment upon the enemies of Israel, they are also types of what will be visited upon the unrepentant sinner of our day.

In Isaiah 32:1,2 the King is reigning and ruling in righteousness. "Behold, a King shall reign in righteousness." Perfect security is shown for His own. A "covert"—a hiding place—of comfort, safety, and blessing for the soul walking with Christ. He is the "shadow of a great rock in a weary land."

Isaiah 35:4-6 is a miracle and a prophecy of Christ as Healer. Miracles of healing were connected with the kingdom testimony, as seen in the Gospels. Matthew alone mentions Christ going forth preaching the gospel of the kingdom.

Isaiah 40:3-5,9,11,12 give the mission of John the Baptist, the forerunner of Christ: "The voice of him that crieth in the wilderness, Prepare ye the way of the Lord." John the Baptist was linked with Old Testament prophecy as shown in the Gospel of Matthew.

> Every valley shall be exalted, and every mountain and hill shall be made low: and the crooked shall be made straight, and the rough places plain . . . and all flesh shall see it together.

In verse nine the writer begins the supreme theme of his prophetic teachings, showing the majestic figure of the coming One.

> O Zion, that bringest good tidings, get thee up into the high mountain; O Jerusalem, that bringest good tidings, lift up thy voice with strength; lift it up, be not afraid; say unto the cities of Judah, Behold your God.

Verse eleven is a type of Christ caring for and preserving the lambs upon His bosom as a mother her babe:[4]

> He shall feed His flock like a shepherd: He shall gather the lambs with His arm, and carry them in His bosom, and shall gently lead those that are with young.

In verse twelve Isaiah is showing that Christ, "measured the waters . . . heaven . . . and weighed the mountains in scales." Here He is mindful of the troubles and privations of His children, and has provided a way to remove them, as a great Burden-Bearer. In the last verse of chapter forty, the Prophet-Christ assures that they, who "wait upon the Lord shall renew [change] their strength; they shall mount up with wings as eagles; they shall run, and not be weary; and they shall walk, and not faint." Here human strength is exchanged for divine. Christ is compared to an "eagle" taking His own through dangers and sorrows amid the journey of life.

In Isaiah 41:18-20 is shown the greatness of Christ, especially toward His own chosen people, as "rivers . . . fountains . . . a pool of water . . . springs of water." The writer is symbolizing the great streams of blessings that come to those thirsting after righteousness. The "cedar, the shittah tree . . . the myrtle . . . the oil tree . . . the fir tree . . . the pine, and the box-tree"—these are symbols of the joy of

4. Isa. 4:3-6; Mal. 3:1; 4:5,6; Matt. 3:3; 11:14,28; Luke 1:17; Isa. 25:9; John 1:18; Matt. 21:42; Eph. 2:20; Isa. 30:33

the Lord that will fill the believer in full fellowship with Himself.[5]

Isaiah 42:1,2,4,19:

Behold my servant, whom I uphold; mine elect, in whom my soul delighteth; I have put my spirit upon him; he shall bring forth judgment to the Gentiles.

This passage pictures Christ as the servant of God, who will reign over the Gentiles, subjects of the kingdom. In verse two He is the servant in meekness and patience: "He shall not cry, nor lift up, nor cause His voice to be heard in the street."

Verse four gives the cure for discouragment: "He shall not fail nor be discouraged." Matthew's Gospel repeats, "Behold my servant whom I have chosen." Christ is portrayed as an ideal, obedient, meek, patient, loyal servant.

Isaiah 43:2:

When thou passeth through the waters, I will be with thee; and through the rivers, they shall not overflow thee.

Christ is found here in assurance and affection when the dark days come.

In Isaiah 45:5,9,22 we find salvation and security only in Christ. His wonderful invitation is also recorded:

I am the Lord, and there is none else . . . Woe unto him that striveth with his Maker . . . Look unto Me, and be ye saved, all the ends of the earth; for I am God, and there is none else.

In Isaiah 48:17 the Jehovah-Lord is the One sent into the world as Redeemer and Guide:

Thus saith the Lord, thy Redeemer, the Holy One of Israel; I am the Lord thy God which teacheth thee

5. Isa. 42:1-4; Matt. 12:17,18; 2 Tim. 1:9

to profit, which leadeth thee by the way that thou shouldest go.[6]

Isaiah 49:16: "Behold, I have graven thee upon the palms of My hands." This indicates Christ's love and tender compassion for His own. The engraving is found in the pierced hands of Calvary.

Isaiah 50:6:

I gave my back to the smiters, and my cheeks to them that plucked off the hair: I hid not my face from shame and spitting.

This tells of the vicarious, sacrificial, substitutionary work of Christ on the Cross. What a price!

Isaiah 52:6: "Therefore My people shall know My name . . . that I AM He." I AM is the name of Deity given to Moses of the JEHOVAH-CHRIST. "I AM that I AM" in Exodus was confirmed in the words of Jesus to the woman at Jacob's well, and to the band sent by the chief priests and Pharisees to arrest Him.[7]

Isaiah 53 is prophetic of Christ in the sufferings at Calvary. It does not refer to the national sufferings of Israel, but to a Person and a Sin-Bearer: "He hath borne our griefs," He "carried our sorrows," "He was wounded for our transgressions," "He was bruised for our iniquities," He made "His soul an offering for sin," "He shall bear their iniquities," "He bare the sins of many," He "made intercession for the transgressors," "The chastisement of our peace was upon Him," "With His stripes we are healed," "The Lord hath laid on Him the iniquity of us all," "For the transgression of My people was He stricken."

These twelve passages show that He hath "appeared to put

6. Isa. 50:6; Matt. 26:67; 27:26; John 18:22; Matt. 12:18-21; Isa. 55:1; Zech. 2:8,11
7. Isa. 52:6; Ex. 3:14; John 4:26; 18:5

away sin by the sacrifice of Himself." "Christ was once offered to bear the sins of many." In this chapter, as in His incarnation, birth, baptism, and passion, we find Christ, the sinless One, identifying Himself with the sinner, that He might put away sin in His own body on the tree. All this is expressed in the Messianic psalm, "the pains of Sheol got hold upon me." We read, "He made His grave with the wicked, and with the rich in His death."

It might be asked why Christ was buried in a rich man's tomb. Christ was crucified according to the Roman custom, which calls for no burial. His body would have remained on the cross for the beasts and elements to destroy. This was not the custom of the Jews. They pled with Pilate that the body might be removed, in which case it would have been interred with the criminals in the common burial place. Joseph of Arimathea prevented this by asking Pilate for the body of Jesus, and laid Him in a newly hewn sepulchre wherein never man lay. The remainder of the verse reads, "He had done no violence, neither was any deceit in His mouth," indicating His holiness and innocence, again foretelling His coming death for others.

The placing of the body of Christ in a clean tomb that had never been defiled, is typically seen at the brazen altar of the Old Testament Tabernacle. Here the *ashes* of the burnt offering represented the dead body of the anti-type, Christ, carried without the camp, and laid in a "clean" place. "He who came from a virgin womb, could only be laid in a virgin tomb."

The following threefold prophecies of Isaiah relative to the crucifixion of Christ have been literally fulfilled:[8]
"He was wounded for our transgressions"—fulfilled in Matthew 27:26,29.

8. Isa. 53; Heb. 9:26,28; Psa. 116:3

"He is brought as a lamb to the slaughter"—fulfilled in Matthew 27:12,14.

"He made His grave with the wicked"—fulfilled in Matthew 27:57-60.

It is interesting to know that Isaiah 53 is no longer read in the Jewish synagogue, while chapters fifty-two and fifty-four are read. Why this omission?

Isaiah 55:1,3 picture Christ in everlasting salvation, with the glorious invitation, "Come unto Me." He also offers the "wine" of joy, and the "milk" of sweetness to His faithful followers.

Isaiah 59:20 refers to Christ's Second Advent. The prophet said:

> The Redeemer shall come to Zion, and unto them that turn from transgressions in Jacob, saith the Lord.

At that time, "Darkness shall cover the earth, and gross darkness the people" (60:2). But the glory breaks forth with, "The glory of the Lord is risen upon thee."

When Jesus began His ministry He was in the synagogue at Nazareth. His first text was from Isaiah 61: "The Spirit of the Lord God is upon Me." Here Christ is the Revealing One to show judgment to the Gentiles.

This chapter begins with the gospel of grace—"The acceptable year of the Lord," which Christ preached at Nazareth. It also records the Second Advent of Christ in judgment, "the day of vengeance of our God."

This and the following chapters of Isaiah foretell the national restoration of Israel to her land, the rejoicing of God's people when the Bridegroom shall come for His bride, and of the reign of Christ. Isaiah gives a threefold picture of the returning Christ as the "King in His beauty," the "Prince

of Peace," and the "King of Righteousness." [9] In Isaiah
64:1-4 the prophet is reviewing the vision of the kingdom
under Jehovah's righteous administration and contemplating
its coming.

9. Isa. 55:1,3,10,13; 59:17; 61; Luke 4:16-21; Isa. 33:17; 9:6; 32:1; Isa.
11:2-5; 40:11; 42:3; 50:6; 53:12; 63:7-9

Chapter 13

CHRIST
and Prophecy

THE OBJECTION OF SOME TO THE STUDY of prophecy, symbols, types, and figurative language, seems most unreasonable. It is stated that more than one-fourth of the Bible is prophetic. If its prophecies are false it can easily be proven. If that is true, what right has the believer to say, "It profiteth nothing?" It is history from Him "who seeth the end from the beginning." Jesus said, "The scripture cannot be broken." Philip could say in assurance, "We have found Him, of whom Moses in the law, and the prophets, did write, Jesus of Nazareth, the son of Joseph."

If the Holy Spirit sees fit to record the future purposes of God, should not the student have a desire to know His teachings? If prophecy is not thoroughly understood we should at least covet the promise:

Blessed is he that readeth, and they that hear the words of this prophecy, and keep those things which are written therein; for the time is at hand.

To understand prophecy correctly Scripture must be compared with Scripture.[1]

No prophecy of the Scripture is of any private interpretation.

To study prophecy prepares for the inevitable—"the doom of things seen, and the blessed hope of things unseen." It is

1. John 1:45; 2 Pet. 1:20; Rev. 1:3

the working out of God's preordained plan. Prophecy draws back the curtain of the future and dispels false security. It is a purifying expectation for those desiring to do His will.

Old Testament prophecy looks down the great vista of the future and sees God's purpose and plan for the ages minutely fulfilled. He who would rightly divide "the Word of truth" will be prepared and undismayed when prophecy becomes history.

Prophecy is the "science of the Bible." The fact of its inspiration is found in the truthfulness of its prophetic interpretation. Prophecy is prewritten history of the nations and especially of the Jews. We should accept the Bible as the written Word of God—that the prophets, inspired of God, recorded for our instruction the history of things to come.

Surely the believer wishes to know the revelation of God's will, mind, and purpose regarding himself and the events to come. Prophecy in the Old Testament is the prewritten history of redemption, with sin and its curse ultimately ended in the glories of Jehovah. At times the two Advents of Christ seem as if without interval between them. The prophets beheld them as in the remote future and almost as simultaneous. One set of prophecies describe Him as coming in humiliation, the other in glory. These prophecies find their reconciliation in the two Advents of Christ. The present gospel age covers this period between the two Advents. Israel rejected His First Advent, as today many reject His Second. The purpose of His return to earth is the establishment of righteousness, and bringing all nations into conformity with its laws.

In studying prophecy in the Old Testament the law of "double reference" should be carefully noted. It is not only *forthtelling* past and present history, but also *foretelling* future history—in types, symbols, and prophecy. Prophecy is the Word of Jehovah with its threefold application:

"Who is and who was and who is to come"—relating to the past, present, and future.[2]

It is stated that none of the sacred writings of the Orient contain prophecy. This is one of the many distinctions of the Bible over the writings of human philosophers, thus proving the inspiration, authenticity, and inerrancy of the Bible. "History is man's dealing with his fellows; the Bible is God's dealing with man."

Prophecy is history foretold, recording the actual events to happen at a certain future time, at certain places, and related to coming world history. It has a beginning, a continuation, and a consummation, recording the past, explaining the present, and predicting the future.[3] "The test of theory is fact; the test of prophecy is its fulfilment," a modern miracle of history.

Dr. David L. Cooper's "Golden Rule of Interpretation" says: "When the plain sense of Scripture makes common sense, seek no other sense; therefore take every word at its primary, ordinary, usual, literal meaning unless the facts of the context indicate clearly otherwise. . . . Avoid every effort to force upon the Scriptures a meaning that is strained and unnatural. Never detach a passage from its context, but always study it carefully in the light of its setting."

Any exposition of prophecy, which is in typical and symbolic language, is exposed to many interpretations unless accompanied by conservative judgment. The student should be careful not to give a mystical, symbolic, or allegorical meaning when the Scripture should be taken at its face value. In the Old Testament the gospel of the New Testament is contained, in prophecy, type, and symbol, foretelling the redemptive facts which were to form the "good tidings."

2. 2 Pet. 1:21
3. Dan. 2:28; 1 Pet. 1:10,11

Fulfilled prophecy proves the plenary inspiration of the Scriptures, God speaking "at sundry times and in divers manners." [4] The prophetic word centers in the sufferings and glories of Christ. The prophecies of His sufferings have been literally fulfilled; those of His manifested glory will be. The Apostle Peter addressing those of the dispersion wrote: [5]

> We have also a more sure word of prophecy; whereunto ye do well that ye take heed, as unto a light that shineth in a dark place, until the day dawn, and the day star arise in your hearts: Knowing this first, that no prophecy of the scripture is of any private interpretation.

The Old Testament Scriptures are divided into the past, present, and future—a trinity pointing to the one complete Christ. Someone has given the illustration as shown in the motion picture: the reel represents the past, that seen the present, and that unseen the future, completing the story.

Prophecy reveals Christ. No man can prophesy; only God can do that because of His foreknowledge. Prophecy cannot be explained as chance. Its predictions are not guesses, nor speculation, but revelation; not concealing, but revealing; not apocryphal, but apocalyptic; not hoary interpretation, but illumination.

The study of prophecy is not only commanded, but it opens up many mysteries ("hidden secrets") of the seen and unseen, for weal or woe. Such are now being rapidly fulfilled. It is the foreshadowing of the revealed mind and purposes of Jehovah, "As a lamp shining in a dark place until the day dawn and the day-star arises." The study of prophecy should be inspiring, instructive, and interesting. Its correct interpretation is not fanatical or farcical, but factual.

4. Heb. 1:1,2
5. 2 Pet. 1:10,19-21; Rev. 1:3; Isa. 26:9; Luke 21:35

It is stated that there are more than two hundred and fifty prophecies in the Old Testament, written from 1000 to 400 B.C., and every one minutely fulfilled. Many of them are most familiar, pertaining to the birth, death, resurrection, and ascension of Christ; 712 years before Christ died on the cross, His death was predicted: "Yet we did esteem Him stricken, smitten of God, and afflicted." [6] If the correctness of this prophecy is questioned, one has but to read the Greek Septuagint (the Hebrew Bible translated into Greek) which was translated 250 years before Christ was born, and which is easily authenticated and established.

For two thousand years Israel looked for her Messiah to come in glory and exaltation. Coming in humiliation He was rejected. However, had He been received by Israel it would have proved that He was not the promised Messiah. It was predicted that He would come to die before He would come in glory.

The Old Testament fully reveals the Second Coming of Christ and His personal reign over the earth. His coming is the "blessed hope" of Israel, of the nations, and of the saints. This will bring peace, blessings, and the fulfilment of that prophecy written above the cross, "Jesus of Nazareth, the King of the Jews."

While Christ is now exalted at the right hand of the Father, there are certain prophecies that are being fulfilled at this moment on the earth. In reference to them, H. L. Mencken, the noted journalist and critic, as well as iconoclast, makes the following observations regarding the present world conditions and Bible prophecies: "All that I desire to point out here is that the New Testament offers precise and elaborate details of the events preceding the

6. Isa. 53:4; John 1:11; Mal. 4:2; Psa. 130:5

inevitable end of the world (age) and that a fair reading of them must lead any rational man to conclude that these events are now upon us. If the Bible is really the Word of God, as we are assured, not only by the Council of Trent, but also by all Protestant authorities, and even the Supreme Court of the United States, then it is plain as day that the human race is on its last legs." Here, of course, Mr. Mencken is referring to the end of this age and prophecies concerning the Second Advent of the Lord.

In the Aramaic phrase used by Paul, *Maranatha* (meaning "our Lord cometh"), the thought is expressed that *Maranatha* was the password of the early Christians. When *Maranatha* becomes a fact then will come to pass: *consummation*, Christ seeing the fruits of His redemption; *satisfaction*, Christ seeing the travail of His soul and being satisfied; *vindication*, Christ's Word, work, and honor vindicated.

In prophecy there is no coincident, no collusion. Its fulfilment is beyond human calculation and comprehension. "The testimony of Christ is the spirit of prophecy." No one can compare prophecies with their fulfilment and not confess their explanation as wholly of God. As the scientist proves the gold by its test, so the fulfilment of prophecy is the proof of its inspiration. The Old Testament prophets looked forward to Bethlehem, Nazareth, Calvary, and Olivet with glowing anticipation. The saints today look backward to them.

To prove the inspiration, authenticity, and inerrancy of the Word of God, some one has listed thirty-two prophecies from the Old Testament, referring to the betrayal, trial, death, and burial of Christ, from several different prophets, and five centuries apart (1000-500 B.C.) which were literally fulfilled within twenty-four hours on the day of the crucifixion of Christ.

B.C.			Prophesied	Fulfilled
487	Sold for 30 pieces of silver	Zech.	11:12	Matt. 26:14,15
487	Money given to the potter	Zech.	11:13	Matt. 27:5-10
487	Side of the Lord pierced	Zech.	12:10	John 19:34-37
487	Forsaken by His disciples	Zech.	13:7	Matt. 26:56
787	Darkness over the earth	Amos	8:9	Matt. 27:45
1047	Christ suffered for all	Psa.	2:1,2	Luke 23:8-12
1047	Christ's forsaken cry	Psa.	22:1	Matt. 27:46
1047	Christ was ridiculed	Psa.	22:7	Matt. 27:41-43
1047	Christ's heart broken	Psa.	22:14	John 19:34
1047	His hands and feet pierced	Psa.	22:16	Luke 23:33
1047	People were astonished	Psa.	22:17	Luke 23:35
1047	Gambled for His vesture	Psa.	22:18	John 19:23,24
1047	His cry of committal	Psa.	31:5	Luke 23:46
1047	Rejected by His own	Psa.	31:11	John 1:11
1047	His bones not broken	Psa.	34:20	John 19:33,36
1047	He was falsely accused	Psa.	35:11	Matt. 26:59,60
1047	Friends were afar off	Psa.	38:11	Luke 23:49
1047	Christ died willingly	Psa.	40:7	John 10:11,17
1047	Betrayed by friends	Psa.	41:9	Matt. 26:49,50
1047	Jesus thirsts	Psa.	69:3	John 19:28-30
1047	Gall and vinegar given	Psa.	69:21	John 19:28,29
1047	Hated without a cause	Psa.	69:4	John 15:25
1047	Judas died, land desolate	Psa.	69:25	Acts 1:16-20
1047	Jesus fell under the cross	Psa.	109:24	John 19:17
1047	People shook their heads	Psa.	109:25	Matt. 27:39
712	Smitten and spit upon	Isa.	50:6	Matt. 27:30
712	His visage marred	Isa.	52:14	Matt. 27:29,30
712	He was wounded and bruised	Isa.	53:5	Matt. 27:26,29
712	He was dumb before accusers	Isa.	53:7	Matt. 27:12,14
712	Buried in rich man's tomb	Isa.	53:9	Matt. 27:57-60
712	Crucified with thieves	Isa.	53:12	Mark 15:27,28
712	Prayed for His persecutors	Isa.	53:12	Luke 23:34

Peter said:

> We have not followed cunningly devised fables, when we made known unto you the power and coming of our Lord Jesus Christ.

The Old Testament Scriptures looked forward to the coming of Christ who should change the world order and thought. He alone can bring order out of chaos today.

Prophecy is not fanaticism nor hallucination, but a vital reality and expectation. The "Day Star" has arisen. The dawn is ushered in by the rising of the sun. In the last chapter of the Old Testament we read:

> But unto you that fear My name shall the Sun of righteousness arise with healing in His wings.

Christ comes to His saints as the dawning of the "Bright and Morning Star." Later, He will burst forth as the Sun in the effulgence of glory.

Christ's Second Coming is foretold in the Old Testament, As the Son of David according to the flesh;[7] To reign over the house of Jacob forever;[8] The Branch shall then build the temple of the Lord;[9] He will rule in glory upon His throne;[10] He will rule as Priest and King;[11] He will reign as Victor with the sceptre;[12] He will reign in righteousness;[13] His divine glory to be manifested in worship;[14] He is coming as Judge.[15]

Previously we listed thirty-two prophecies of the arrest, trial, and crucifixion of the Lord literally fulfilled within twenty-four hours after His arrest. Without repeating these we are giving other prophecies from the Old Testament relating to Christ:

Prophesied B.C.		Old Testament		New Testament	
4000	To be the "Seed" of a woman........	Gen.	3:15	Matt.	1:1
712	To be born of a virgin.............	Isa.	7:14	Matt.	1:23
4000	To be a Jew......................	Gen.	12:3	Matt.	1:1
712	Birth to be miraculous.............	Isa.	9:6	Matt.	1:18-25
1000	To be of the house of David........	Psa.	132:11	Rom.	1:3
710	To be born at Bethlehem...........	Mic.	5:2	Matt.	2:1-6
4000	To be of the tribe of Judah.........	Gen.	49:10	Matt.	2:6
1451	To be a Prophet...................	Deut.	18:18	Acts	3:22
606	To make a New Covenant..........	Jer.	31:31,33	Heb.	8:7
712	A light to all nations..............	Isa.	49:6	Luke	2:30-32
520	Riding on an ass..................	Zech.	9:9	Matt.	21:1-7
742	To be a stumbling block............	Isa.	8:14	1 Cor.	1:23
698	To perform miracles...............	Isa.	61:1,2	Matt.	11:2-6
1000	Rejected by the rulers.............	Psa.	118:22,23	Acts	4:11
758	Christ's teachings rejected..........	Isa.	6:9,10	Matt.	13:14
600	Cleansing of the Temple............	Jer.	7:6	Matt.	21:13

7. Psa. 132:11; Dan. 7:13,14; Acts 1:6,7; 2:30
8. Isa. 9:6,7; 24:23; Ezek. 34:23,24; 37:24,25; Mic. 4:7; 5:2; Acts 15:16
9. Zech. 6:12,13; Jer. 23:5,6; 30:9; Isa. 9:3; 32:1; 33:17
10. Isa. 6:1,3; Zech. 6:13; 9:9,10; John 12:41
11. Jer. 33:17; 23:5,6; 30:9; Ezek. 37:24-28; Hag. 2:9; Isa. 52:7; Hos. 3:5
12. Gen. 49:10; Num. 24:17; Psa. 2:6-9; 24:8; 45:3-6; 72:5-11; 89:2-29; Isa. 40:10; Mic. 5:2; Dan. 2:35,44; 9:25; 7:13; 8:23; Hos. 3:5
13. Isa. 32:1; 49:7
14. Isa. 2:2-3; 4:5,6; 60:10; 66:18-23; Jer. 3:17; Zech. 8:20; 14:16
15. Psa. 72:2,4; 75:2; 96:13; 110:6; Isa. 2:4; 11:3,4; Mic. 4:3; 5:1; **Mal.** 3:2; 2 Sam. 23:3; Zech. 9:9

Prophesied B.C.		*Old Testament*		*New Testament*	
520	Betrayed for 30 pieces of silver.......	Zech.	11:12	Matt.	26:14,15
520	Christ's shepherds scatter...........	Zech.	13:7	Matt.	26:56
520	Looked upon when pierced..........	Zech.	12:10	John	19:24-30
740	As babe carried into Egypt..........	Hosea	11:1	Matt.	2:15
1520	The promised Redeemer.............	Job	19:25	Gal.	4:4
712	To come to His own................	Isa.	40:3	Luke	3:4
712	Rejected by His own................	Isa.	53:3	John	1:11
1047	Christ's death set forth.............	Psa.	22:14	John	19:16
712	Christ's burial foretold.............	Isa.	53:9	Matt.	27:57
1047	Christ's resurrection foretold........	Psa.	16:10	Acts	2:24-33
1047	Christ's ascension predicted.........	Psa.	110:1	Acts	7:55
487	Second coming prophesied..........	Zech.	14:4-8; Isa.		2:1-4
712	Christ's exaltation foretold..........	Isa.	66:1; Psa.	118:22	

WHAT HAPPENS WHEN JESUS COMES AGAIN?

All the families of the earth shall be blest;[1]
The heathen given to Christ for an inheritance;[2]
"All . . . the nations shall worship before thee";[3]
"All the earth . . . shall sing unto thee";[4]
"Kings shall fall down before Him";[5]
"Righteousness and peace have kissed each other";[6]
"Glorious things are spoken of thee";[7]
Thy throne shall endure forever;[8]
Heavens will rejoice;[9]
"Neither shall they learn war any more";[10]
"Peace shall know no end";[11]
"Death swallowed up in victory";[12]
Cleavage of the Mt. of Olives;[13]
Meeting of Christ and saved in the air;[14]

1. Gen. 12:3
2. Psa. 2:8
3. Psa. 22:27,31; 86:9; 138:4,5
4. Psa. 66:4; 68:31
5. Psa. 72:5-17
6. Psa. 85:10-12
7. Psa. 87:1-5
8. Psa. 89:35
9. Psa. 96:11-13
10. Isa. 2:2-5; 41:2,3
11. Isa. 9:7; 11:6-10
12. Isa. 25:6-8; 29:18,19; 32:15-17; 35:1,2; 40:5; 42:3,4; 45:8; 51:6-8; Isa. 53:10-12; 54:1-3; 55:5-13; 60:1-9; 66:12-23; Hab. 2:14; Hag. 2:7; Zech. 2:10,11; 14:8-21; Mal. 1:11
13. Zech. 14:4
14. John 14:3; 1 Thess. 4:14

Redemption of the glorified bodies in resurrection;[15]
Saints rewarded for faithful service;[16]
Perfection of sight and spiritual knowledge;[17]
Freedom from sin and Satan;[18]
Renovation of the physical earth;[19]
Saints sharing in the glory of Christ;[20]
Restoration of Israel's national glory;[21]
Golden Age of peace on the earth.[22]

15. Phil. 3:20,21
16. 1 Cor. 3:11,14
17. 1 Cor. 13:12
18. Rev. 20:1,2
19. Rom. 8:20-22
20. Matt. 13:43
21. Hosea 3:5
22. Rev. 20:1-6

Chapter 14

CHRIST
the Shepherd

IN THE OLD TESTAMENT WE FIND CHARacters that are the shepherd-type of Christ. These types show the character as well as the devotion and duties of the Shepherd. He is shown as the "Good," "Great," and "Chief" Shepherd.

The Good Shepherd points back to the Cross, to the Prophet;
The Great Shepherd looks up to the Throne, to the Priest;
The Chief Shepherd looks forward to His coming, the King.

In the 22nd Psalm the Good Shepherd purchases His sheep;
In the 23rd Psalm the Great Shepherd defends His sheep;
In the 24th Psalm the Chief Shepherd rewards His sheep.

The Good Shepherd came first as Prophet-Saviour, to die;
The Great Shepherd now as Priest-Intercessor, intercedes;
The Chief Shepherd as coming King-Judge, rewards His faithful.

Ezekiel gives a prophetic designation of Jehovah as the "Shepherd of Israel," gathering together the outcasts of His own chosen people:

As a shepherd seeketh out his flock in the day that he is among his sheep that are scattered; so will I seek out my sheep, and will deliver them out of all places where they have been scattered in the cloudy and dark day.

The book of Psalms is Israel's song book, and for years they had sung, "Jehovah-Ro'i is my Shepherd" . . . "Give ear, O Shepherd of Israel, thou that leadest Joseph like a flock." When Jesus announced Himself as the "Good Shepherd," it was a declaration that He had come as the promised Deliverer to set His people free.

Sheep never find rest until satisfied with food. Neither can the believer apart from the Good, Great, and Chief Shepherd of the flock. Psalms is a collection of inspired prayers and songs, devotional and eminently prophetic. They reveal the sufferings of Jehovah and the coming glory.

God's judgment fell upon the Shepherd-Saviour on Calvary that the sheep might be delivered: "Smite the Shepherd, and the sheep shall be scattered." Christ has no more divine type than the "Good Shepherd." There is no self-sacrifice greater than His on Calvary.[1]

In the Song of Solomon we have a picture of the Shepherd separated from the beautiful Shulamite. She cries,

> Until the day break, and the shadows flee away, turn, my beloved, and be thou like the roe or a young hart upon the mountains of Bether.

The word "Bether" means separation. The Shepherd-Bridegroom is now separated from His bride "until the day break."

Abel was the first shepherd-type of Christ:

> And to the blood of sprinkling, that speaketh better things than that of Abel.

Here we have the sin-offering of Leviticus for the forgiveness of sin, which typifies the blood of the Good Shepherd. Abel offered a lamb, the lamb dying for the shepherd. Christ, the Shepherd on the Cross, died for His lambs.[2] In the Old

---

1. John 10:11; Heb. 13:20; 1 Pet. 5:4; Psa. 45; 46:6-9; 22; 23; 24; Ezek. 34:12; Zech. 13:7; Isa. 53:3-7; Matt. 26:31; Gen. 49:24; Psa. 80:1
2. Heb. 12:24; Gen. 4:10,11

Testament the sheep died for the shepherd; in the New Testament the Shepherd died for the sheep.

Isaac, the wealthy shepherd:

> The Lord hath blessed my master greatly . . . with flocks and herds.

This wealthy shepherd is a type of Christ, the Good Shepherd, finding His riches in His saints. They are to be a praise and glory to Him throughout the ages. This is why He carefully keeps His own. Paul says they are "the riches of the glory of His inheritance." Moses sings, "For the Lord's portion is in His people." The sheep are precious in the sight of the Shepherd. It is the Shepherd that seeks the sheep, and not the sheep that seek the Shepherd.[3]

Jacob, the responsible shepherd, shows his responsibility to Laban:

> That which was torn of beasts I brought not unto thee; I bare the loss.

Christ, the Good Shepherd, makes Himself responsible for His sheep. Jacob did lose some, but this will not be true of the anti-type, Christ. As the shepherds of the East kept watch by day and night, so will the heavenly Shepherd care for His sheep:

> He that keepeth thee will not slumber. Behold, He that keepeth Israel shall neither slumber nor sleep.

The Jacob-Shepherd journeyed for a wife:

> Jacob fled into the country of Syria, and Israel served for a wife, and for a wife he kept sheep.

So the Christ-Shepherd, as the Son of man, came as a servant. He will ultimately claim His bride.

The first time the "hands" of the Christ-Shepherd are

3. Gen. 18:12; 24:35; 37:8-20

mentioned in the Bible is in connection with the shepherd-Jacob:

> The hands of the mighty God of Jacob; (from thence is the shepherd, the stone of Israel.)

Joseph was the hated shepherd, and by his own brother-shepherds:

> Shalt thou indeed reign over us? . . . And they hated him yet the more.

Christ, the Good Shepherd, was hated by His shepherd-brethren. The Sanhedrin, Pharisees, Scribes, and Sadducees, neglecting their flock (Israel), proved themselves to be false shepherds. The Old Testament tells of the false prophets who existed then as well as today:

> Thy shepherds slumber . . . thy people is scattered . . . no man gathereth them. Therefore they went their way as a flock, they were troubled, because there was no shepherd. Mine anger was kindled against the shepherd that leaveth the flock.

Ezekiel prophesied against those unfaithful shepherds, and God says;

> I will set up one Shepherd over them, and He shall feed them, even my servant David.

Christ saw the people "as sheep having no shepherd." He came to lead them into green pastures.[4]

Moses was the leader-shepherd :

> He led the flock to the back side of the desert.

For forty years Moses was a shepherd for Jethro's flock, preparing later to shepherd God's flock. For forty years he was leading God's flock toward the promised land, Canaan:

---

4. Gen. 30:31-43; 33:13; Eph. 1:18; Hosea 12:12; 2 Tim. 1:12; 1 Pet. 1:5; Psa. 121:4; Isa. 40:11; Luke 22:27

Then he remembered the days of old, Moses and his people; saying, Where is he that brought them up out of the sea with the shepherd of the flock?

Christ is the great anti-type of Moses, who "goeth before them, and the sheep follow Him." [5]

David was the shepherd-king and deliverer. As such he rescued the lamb from the mouth of the bear. Christ, the Good Shepherd, leaves the safe ninety and nine and goes after the one that is lost. Eliab said to David, "With whom hast thou left those few sheep in the wilderness?" David left them with the keeper. Christ, the Shepherd-Keeper, has left His own with the Holy Spirit in this age. It is through the indwelling Spirit that Christ expects His under-shepherds to "feed the flock of God." [6]

The false and good Shepherd are contrasted in John 10:

FALSE SHEPHERD	GOOD SHEPHERD
Entereth not by the door, verse 1.	Entereth in by the door, verse 2.
A stranger will they not follow, verse 5.	The sheep follow Him; for they know His voice, verse 4.
But will flee from him, verse 5 (Some other way).	Verily, verily . . . I am the door, verse 7 (I am the way).
Cometh not, but for to steal, kill, destroy, verse 10.	I am come that they might have life, verse 10.
Is an hireling, verse 12 (tramp laborer).	He giveth His life for the sheep, verse 11.
Seeth the wolf coming, and leaveth, verse 12.	I lay down My life for the sheep, verse 15.
He hath a devil, and is mad, verse 20.	Can a devil open the eyes of the blind? verse 21.
If thou be the Christ, tell us plainly, verse 24.	Ye are not of My sheep, verse 26.

5. Ex. 3:1-12; Isa. 63:11,12; Luke 15:4; 1 Sam. 17:34; 1 Chr. 17:7
6. Ezek. 34:2,23,25; Zech. 11:17; Gal. 4:28,29; John 9:16; 10:4,16

FALSE SHEPHERD	GOOD SHEPHERD
Then the Jews took up stones again to stone Him, verse 31.	For which of those works do ye stone Me? verse 32.
But for blasphemy . . . makest thyself God? verse 33.	Whom the Father hath sanctified . . . Thou blasphemest, verse 36.

Chapter 15

CHRIST
and Isaac

ISAAC WAS THE PROPHESIED "SEED." Abraham laughed with exultant joy at the thought of a son in whom the everlasting Covenant was to be established. Ishmael, child of the bondwoman, was not to be the son of promise. He is today the ancestor of the Arabs and Mohammedans, enemies of Israel, numbering over one hundred and fifty million. Christians are the spiritual seed of Abraham by faith in Jesus Christ. The legalists, the seed of the bondwoman, are supplementing faith by works of the law.[1]

It was on Mount Moriah ("sacred hill") that Abraham offered Isaac, both types of God the Father and His only begotten Son. It was on Mount Moriah that David interceded for his people. Here King Solomon built the Temple to Jehovah.

Many brides mentioned in the Old Testament are types of the bride of Christ. Here the true believer, woven into prophecy, suggests the *oneness* with their Lord. The stories of Rebekah, Rachel, and Ruth, the brides of Isaac, Jacob, and Boaz, are beautiful types. Ruth, the Gentile bride, became the ancestress of Jesus.

As Adam sought his bride "in the cool of the day" (evening); as the servant of Abraham, when seeking the bride for Isaac, had his camels kneel by the well of water "at the time of the evening"; and when Isaac meditating in the field "at the eventide" saw his espoused bride coming; so this

1. Gen. 17:16-19; 18:12; Gal. 4:28,29

present age may now be in its "eventide" when Christ will be coming for His bride. What a glorious day that will be!

Isaac lived 180 years (1896-1716 B.C.) and was a beautiful type of Christ.[2]

Isaac was supernaturally born, the only son of promise;
Was hated by his brother without a cause;
Was submissive to his father's will, and condemned to die;
Was humble, pious, full of faith, and obedient unto death;
Was a foreshadowed substitute, and saw the need of a lamb;
Was a sacrifice provided, bearing the wood for the sacrifice;
Was placed on the altar, but expected to be raised by his father.

Isaac was hidden three days from sight; Christ was hidden three days in Sheol but was received back by the Father;

Isaac was seeking a bride: Christ is selecting His bride;

Isaac prepared a journey for his bride: Christ is coming to meet His bride.

Isaac's Rebekah waited in purity; Christ's bride will be without spot.

Isaac sent gifts to his bride; Christ will reward His faithful.

Isaac manifested himself to his bride: so will Christ at His coming.

Isaac was awaiting his bride; so Christ awaits His bride.

Isaac lifted up his eyes and saw his bride; Christ will see His bride adorned at His coming.

Isaac met his bride at eventide; Christ will meet His bride at the close of this age.

Isaac was acceptable to her kin; so will Christ be at His coming.

Isaac's father arranged the marriage; Christ's heavenly Father is arranging for the Son's.

Rebekah was left free to say "I will go"; Christ's bride was left a free moral agent to accept Him.

2. Gen. 21:24 to 35:29

Chapter 16

CHRIST
and Joseph

JOSEPH IS ONE OF THE FEW BIBLE CHAR-acters of whom no word of condemnation is written. He was brought from prison walls to be the grand-vizier of Egypt. Like his anti-type, Christ, Joseph was used in saving many human lives by the provision made for them. His faith, piety, patience, and self-control give a beautiful picture of a young man in whom there is no guile.

Bible students have given many points of resemblance between the history of Joseph and that of Christ.[1]

JOSEPH	CHRIST
The shepherd, feeding his flock.	"I Am the Good Shepherd."
Beloved of his father.	"This is My beloved Son, in whom I am well pleased."
Hated by his brothers.	"They have hated Me without a cause."
Not believed by his brothers.	Neither did His brethren believe in Him.
Not allowed to reign over his brothers.	"We will not have this man to reign over us."
Envied by his brothers.	The chief priests delivered Him for envy.

1. Gen. 37:2-36; 39:1-23; 41:14-56; 42:7-25; 43:16; 45:1-26; John 1:11,29; John 2:5,24,25; 3:35; 5:19; 6:68; 7:5; 10:11; 15:25; Heb. 4:15; 13:20; Matt. 2:14,15; 3:17; 10:32; 11:28,29; 22:4; 26:16; 27:1,2,28,36; Luke 1:33; 3:23; 9:58; 15:14; 19:10,14,41; 17:17; 23:32,43; 24:11,31,39; Mark 15:10; 1 Pet. 5:4; 1 John 3:2; 4:9; Eccl. 4:14; Hosea 11:1; Phil. 2:7,10; Phil. 4:19; Eph. 1:3; 1 Cor. 11:24; Acts 9:5; 10:38

JOSEPH	CHRIST
Became a wanderer in the field.	"The Son of man hath not where to lay His head."
"I seek my brethren."	Came to seek and to save that which was lost.
They conspired against him.	They took counsel against Jesus to put Him to death.
They stripped Joseph.	They stripped Him, and put on Him a scarlet robe.
They sat down . . . and looked.	Sitting down they watched Him there.
Sold for 20 pieces of silver.	They covenanted for 30 pieces of silver.
Sold into Egypt.	"Out of Egypt have I called My Son."
A servant of Potiphar.	Took upon Him the form of a servant.
Potiphar put everything into his hands.	The Father hath given all things into His hand.
The Lord blessed for Joseph's sake.	Hath blessed us with all spiritual riches in Christ.
"How can I do this great wickedness against God?"	Was in all points tempted . . . yet without sin.
Put him into prison, bound.	And when they had bound Him, they led Him away.
Pharaoh was wroth against two—butler and baker.	And there were also two others, malefactors.
His message of life to one.	"Today shalt thou be with Me in paradise."
"But think on me."	"This do in remembrance of Me."
"Make mention of me."	"Whosoever shall confess Me."
But they forgot him.	"But where are the nine?"
They brought him hastily out of the dungeon.	Out of prison He cometh to reign.
"It is not in me."	The Son can do nothing of Himself.
A man in whom the Spirit of God is.	God anointed Jesus with the Holy Ghost and with power.

JOSEPH	CHRIST
"According unto thy word shall all my people be ruled."	"He shall reign over the house of Jacob for ever."
They cried before him, "Bow the knee."	At the name of Jesus every knee shall bow.
Joseph was 30 years old.	Jesus began to be about 30 years of age.
Pharaoh said, "Go unto Joseph."	Peter said to the Lord, "To whom shall we go?"
"What he saith to you, do."	"Whatsoever He saith unto you, do it."
The famine was over all the face of the earth.	A mighty famine was in that land.
Took to himself a Gentile bride.	Will take unto Himself a Gentile bride.
Exalted, positionally, next to the king, Pharaoh.	As King, exalted at the right hand of the Father.
He knew his brothers.	Knew all men.
They knew not him.	The world knew Him not.
He turned and wept.	He beheld the city and wept.
Filled their sacks.	Shall supply all your need.
"Bring these men home."	"Come unto the marriage supper."
Made himself known.	Their eyes were opened, and they knew Him.
"I am your brother, whom ye sold."	"I am Jesus whom thou persecutest."
"Behold, your eyes see."	"Behold My hands and My feet."
"Come down unto me."	"Come unto Me . . . and I will give you rest."
Jacob's heart fainted, for he believed them not.	The apostles and women believed Him not.
Suffered for the sake of others.	"Father, forgive them; for they know not what they do."
Presented his brothers to the king.	Will present His glorified saints "without spot."

JOSEPH	CHRIST
Brought his brothers to repentance.	"I am not come to call the righteous, but sinners to repentance."
Provided salvation of the body for nothing.	Provides salvation of the soul through free grace.
After the humiliation, came the exaltation.	After the Cross, came the crown.
Received a coat of many colors.	Gives a robe of His righteousness.
Left the vale of Hebron for his brethren.	Left the glory of the Father for His brethren.
Was delivered by one of his brethren, Reuben.	Was betrayed by one of His apostles, Judas.
Was cast into the pit to die.	Was nailed to the Cross to die.
Had a kid killed as a substitute.	Was the Lamb killed as our Substitute.
Received an invitation to come to Pharaoh.	Invites sinners to come unto Him and rest.
Was made the head of Pharaoh's house.	Is made the Head of the church, His body.
Was given a seat on Pharaoh's throne.	Is now seated on His Father's throne.
Received the signet ring of authority.	"All power is given unto Me."

Chapter 17

CHRIST
and Moses

(Hebrew, *mosheh*, To draw out)

THE SECRET OF MOSES' ENDURANCE WAS that, in faith, "he endured, as seeing Him who is invisible." Even in old age his eye was not dim nor his natural force abated. Faith upheld him. Moses was a type of Christ in his prophetic office, as a great teacher and wonder-worker, and willing to be "blotted out" for the sake of his brethren.

Moses is often referred to as "the man of God." This title occurs 78 times in the Old Testament and twice in the New. It was first used of Moses who was a prophet, a spokesman for God:[1]

And this is the blessing, wherewith Moses the man of God blessed the children of Israel before his death.

Moses wrote of Christ in the Pentateuch:

For had ye believed Moses, ye would have believed Me; for he wrote of Me.

Christ was the Prophet, the Faithful Witness, because He spoke the things given Him by the Father.

In the birth of Moses he was the promised deliverer, to be the prophet of faith. Like his anti-type, Christ, he was rejected by his own. As Christ was tested three times by Satan, so was Moses tested forty years in Egypt, forty years in the

1. Deut. 33:1; Ex. 4:8; Heb. 11:27

land of Midian, and forty years leading Israel from bondage. The number forty is the number of testing.

Thomas Guthrie has said: "Take Moses for and in all, regard him not as one, but in many respects, he is the greatest character in history, sacred or profane."

Stephen speaks of Moses as being separated unto God ("fair unto God") to an appointed calling. Here the sovereignty of God is seen at the beginning of the life of Moses.

The name "Moses" appears 700 times in the Bible, 37 times in the Gospels. As a type of Christ note the following comparisons:[2]

MOSES	CHRIST
Struck the fetters from millions of slaves.	Has delivered millions from the slavery of sin.
Reduced the people to order, controlling and subduing them.	Will bring all things into subjection and unto Himself.
Formed a great nation from base, enslaved material.	Will form His kingdom from sinners "saved by grace."
Inaugurated human laws and government.	Will rule with divine laws of justice and righteousness.
Gave criminal, civil, and sanitary laws, a pattern to the world.	Provides a new heaven and earth free from sickness and death.
Was a great lawgiver, guide, organizer, liberator, soldier.	Is the perfect guide, lawgiver, preserver, liberator.
Came twice to Israel.	Has come once, and will come the second time to the earth.
Took a Gentile bride.	Is preparing a bride, the Church.

2. Ex. 3:10; 7:1; 33:18; 4:27; 5:1; 1 John 3:2; Ex. 2:21; 1 Thess. 4:13-16; Ex. 17:6; Acts 7:19-23; Isa. 7:14; 9:6; Ex. 2:21; Eph. 1:22-23; 5:32; Deut. 18:15-19; John 1:45; 1:11; Ex. 2:14; Ex. 2:16; John 4:6; Eph. 2:8; Ex. 2:17; John 10:11; Luke 19:41; Ex. 2:4-8; Matt. 2:20; Acts 7:37; John 4:10; Zech. 12:10; 13:6; Num. 21:8; John 3:14,15; Ex. 3:8; 16:15; John 6:31-34

MOSES	CHRIST
Saw the glory of God.	Reveals the glory of God.
Was a faithful shepherd.	Is the Good, Great, and Chief Shepherd.
Was Israel's deliverer.	Is the Deliverer of the saints.
Was the lowly babe from the bulrushes.	Was the lowly babe in the manger.
Held in his hand the rod of power.	"All power is given unto Me."
Took hold of a serpent.	Will cast the serpent into the lake of fire.
Took the rod of power and government into his own hands.	Will take power at His Second Coming, and end Satan's dominion.
Carried the message of God to Pharaoh.	Brought the message of God to the world.
Was raised up as a prophet of God.	Was "that prophet" foretold by Moses and the law.
Was not wanted by his own.	Came unto His own, and His own received Him not.
Sat at the well of Midian.	Sat at the well of Jacob.
Made a covenant purely of grace.	Has made a covenant of grace with His believers.
Was rejected and the sorrows of Israel increased.	Was rejected by Israel and her sorrows increased.
His life as a babe was sought by Pharaoh.	His life as a babe was sought by Herod.
Established the law.	Fulfilled the law.
Brought forth living water.	Is the living water.
Gave the bread from heaven.	Is the manna from heaven.
Points to the saviour lifted up, in the wilderness.	Is the Saviour lifted up on the Cross.

Chapter 18

CHRIST
in the Book of Joshua

IT IS STATED THAT THE "OLD TESTAment foreshadows the New, and the New Testament unfolds the Old," namely;

Genesis, the beginning, foreshadows Matthew, the beginning of a new dispensation;

Exodus, the going out, foreshadows redemption and deliverance, as unfolded in Acts and Romans;

Numbers, the wanderings of an earthly people, foreshadowing Philippians, showing the path of a heavenly people;

Psalms and the prophets, foreshadowing Revelation, the prophetic book of the New Testament;

Joshua, foreshadowing Ephesians, the highest revelation of spiritual living, in the most holy place with Christ.

The book of Joshua (Hebrew, *Joshua*, Greek, *Jesus*, Jehovah is salvation) gives the picture of Israel passing through the river Jordan in order to reach Canaan. Jordan, the river of death, is a type of Calvary; Canaan a type of resurrection, and victory. Jordan (Hebrew, *Jared*) means "to descend." (*Mahaleel-Jared*, "The blessed God who descends.")

Canaan is not a type of heaven. There are no wars nor death in heaven. Canaan typifies a victorious, overcoming, resurrection life of the believer on earth, a foretaste of the heavenly life to come.

Types are but shadows of the real substance:

Now all these things happened unto them for ensamples: and they are written for our admonition, upon whom the ends of the world are come.

The first type we find in the book of Joshua is divine grace:

The land which I do give to them—Goodly and large, flowing with milk and honey.

Israel was a "stiff-necked people," but Jehovah showed His divine grace toward them in giving them the land:

Every place that the sole of your foot shall tread upon, that have I given unto you, as I said unto Moses.

Here was possession by entering, through the grace of God. Israel failed to appreciate the gift; she never took Lebanon. How sad it is that so many of God's children fail to appreciate the blessings of grace. Both Israel and Christians are "chosen in grace." The Israelites were an earthly people; Christians a heavenly; Israel had an earthly Jerusalem, Christians will have a New Jerusalem; Israel received her earthly blessings, Christians their heavenly. "Possession is heart occupation; faith is appropriation." Even now the Christian should "sit in the heavenlies in Christ Jesus," finding the "unsearchable riches of Christ." The weakness of the believer is in not "possessing his possessions."

Christ calls for a separated people. This came at Jordan:

That the waters which came down from above stood and rose up upon an heap very far from the city . . . and the people passed over right against Jericho. ("Place of fragrance")

Israel never entered Canaan (a type of rest) until after passing through Jordan (a type of death to self). Followers of Christ should leave Egypt (type of the world), hasten through the wilderness (type of a defeated follower), pass over the "river of death" (in self-abnegation), and enter Canaan, the promised land of victory, power, prayer, and plenty.

> Thou wilt keep him in perfect peace, whose mind is stayed on thee: because he trusteth in Thee. Trust ye in the Lord forever: for in the Lord Jehovah is everlasting strength.

Jehovah wanted this separated people to be occupied with Himself. This was the reason for observing feasts and holy days, that they might not contact the idol worshipers. Christ would have the believer find in Him his Sabbath-rest, as a type of Israel's Canaan-rest promised to Abraham. Joshua also desired a separated people, death to the flesh, as typified in circumcision. Joshua saw the "reproach of Egypt taken away." Christ sees the believer delivered, raised, and seated, positionally, with Himself in glory.

Joshua, typically through death and resurrection, brought Israel from Egypt to Canaan. Christ, through death and resurrection, provides a Canaan-life for His own. Joshua heard the assuring words, "I will not fail thee, nor forsake thee." Christ says, "Follow Me . . . whosoever shall lose his life for My sake and the gospel's, the same shall save it."

Joshua led his people through Jordan (river of death) to ascend on the other side. Christ went through Jordan (death), descended into the grave, and arose from the grave. Joshua placed twelve stones in Jordan. Christ was "that Rock," smitten in death. Joshua provided a new way: "Ye have not passed this way heretofore." Christ provides a new way: "I Am the way."

The book of Joshua cites the cities of refuge, three cities on either side of Jordan. These were God's appointed shelters from the avenger. The priest stood at the gate ready to receive the sinner. The writer to the Hebrews says we "have fled for refuge to lay hold upon the hope set before us."

God, in grace, has provided a refuge for the sinner in Christ. As Prophet-Priest He awaits at heaven's door to receive the penitent who is saved by His marvelous grace. Christ is the provision originating in the divine love of God, for the sinner's every need.[1]

1. 1 Cor. 10:11; Rom. 15:4; 2 Tim. 3:16,17; Joshua 1:2; Deut. 9:6; Eph. 2:8; Rom. 6:6-11; Phil. 3:21; 4:19; John 10:10; Isa. 26:3,4; Ex. 34:10-26; Deut. 5:12-15; Matt. 12:1,11; Mark 1:21; 2:21; 2:23; 3:2; Luke 4:16; 13:10; Acts 13:14; 16:13; Heb. 6:18; Joshua 20

Chapter 19

CHRIST
and Eschatology

WE ARE LIVING IN THE GREATEST DRAMA of the past two thousand years. Many think we are living in the "evening" of this present age, and in the remaining years changes will take place with even greater speed.

The Jew was familiar with the word "kingdom." The expression "kingdom of heaven" is found only in Matthew's Gospel, applying especially to the Jew. It was a great key-word to the ardent Jew. Their national hope was in Israel's Messiah, their King, seed of Abraham, and the establishment of a world-wide kingdom. Jesus did not rebuke His disciples after His crucifixion for asking, "Lord, wilt Thou at this time restore again the kingdom to Israel?" This was the dominating thought of their hearts.

The Old Testament prophets, Christ, and the apostles, spoke of the kingdom of heaven as future, connecting it with another age. Admittedly, that kingdom has not come, but is in formation. The petition of the model prayer of Jesus was, "Thy kingdom come." If the kingdom is not to be realized now, with present believers subjects of it, then it can only be consummated in the appearance of the Messiah-Christ. The present order of things on the earth cannot imply the kingdom, for Christ says, "My kingdom is not of this world."

Men from the days of Adam to the present have been looking for a brighter day, the golden age of the Old Testament. Plato envisaged a social utopia in his noted dialogue, the *Republic*, which since has been marred by human greed, strife, and war. Pseudo-statesmen would adopt it today with the United Nations organization. Nations seem to reject the leadership of Jesus Christ, who came to bring life, light, and freedom to a sin-cursed race. The late Franklin D. Roosevelt in one of his "fireside chats" proposed a "New World Order" for the realization of a world utopia. He stated, "This is no vision of a distant millennium, but a definite basis for a kind of world obtainable in our time and generation." But no nation, or nations, can function properly apart from Christ. An idealistic and unrealistic man-made utopia will not produce a millennium. Only the Prince of Peace can bring in a reign of peace. Such will not be universal until Christ's reign of righteousness is established on the earth.

Milton tried to change *Paradise Lost* into a *Paradise Regained*, but it has failed during these six thousand years of "man's day." Sir Thomas More's *Utopia* wrote of that beautiful imaginary island, but it has never been found. Such a millennium cannot be evolved by human planning. Sir Walter Raleigh sought it in the new world of Virginia. The Pilgrim fathers came to New England to avoid persecution, but became persecutors themselves. Thomas Paine wrote his *Age of Reason* as a panacea for the evils of the world, which is ending in moral chaos. The late Woodrow Wilson's slogan was, "Make the world safe for democracy," when the world needed a theocracy, *God*. Many would claim that education and evolution would evolve into a millennium, but devolution and social putrefaction have ensued. Evil is evil. The years of World War Two witnessed the greatest desolation in human history. This world must be in its twilight. The prayer of the saints should be, "Come quickly, Lord Jesus, come quickly." Only at His coming will the problems of the universe find solution.

Regarding events after the First Coming of Christ, the Old Testament emphasis is upon the future age of glory. The New Testament deals with the blessings in "the heavenlies," while the Old Testament deals with the deliverances and glory to come. It is said that there are 333 prophecies in the Old Testament referring to the First Coming of Christ to Israel, and that there are 333 prophecies in the New Testament referring to the Second Coming of Christ to the nations.

This golden age was revealed to Abraham and through him "all the families of the earth [would] be blessed"; to Isaac as "an everlasting covenant"; and to the tribe of Judah, saying,

> The scepter shall not depart . . . until Shiloh come; and unto Him shall the gathering of the people be.

The restoration of Israel is seen in the covenant made with Abram and recorded in Genesis. This is an unconditional promise to Abram and to his descendants. "The gifts and calling of God are without repentance." In Deuteronomy 28:13 is the promise that Israel shall become the "head" and not the "tail" of nations. In Acts we are shown that the tabernacle of David shall be rebuilt. This cannot be done "until the times of the Gentiles be fulfilled," and God has gathered His elect from the nations of the earth.

Zechariah tells of Israel's moral repentance and restoration which is emphasized by Paul in his letter to the Corinthians. Ezekiel also records the restoration of the tribes of Israel. United to the house of Judah they shall again become one nation. With these twelve reunited tribes God makes a New Covenant, as seen in Jeremiah and Isaiah. Even now Jerusalem is practically being rebuilt, an earnest of what is to follow. Israel is seen returning to Palestine in great numbers and wealth, all of which was prophesied eight hundred years before Christ was born. These prophecies have been only partially fulfilled.

Joshua entered Canaan, but under the covenant of law, which was to continue upon obedience to God, as recorded by Moses. Israel failed and ultimately was sent into captivity, with only a remnant returning. To the "lost sheep of Israel" Jesus Christ finally came. By them He was rejected. Since Titus destroyed Jerusalem a few years later, the Jews have been a homeless nation, yet retaining their national identity.

Of the House of David it was said, "I will establish the throne of His kingdom for ever." It was prophesied by Isaiah that, "A virgin shall conceive . . . a son." This Son was to "reign over the House of Jacob for ever; and of His kingdom there shall be no end."

The dominant theme and central doctrine of the apocalyptic books of the Old Testament is the universal rule and reign of Christ, with Israel being to a great degree the medium of Messianic blessing to all nations. This expectation pervaded the Gentile as well as the Jewish mind.

The first prophecy of a universal King and kingdom to be established is mentioned in the words of Nathan the prophet, in the Davidic covenant, "I will establish the throne of His kingdom forever." This was confirmed by the Lord to David:[1]

> I will raise up thy seed after thee, which shall be of thy sons; and I will establish His kingdom . . . I will settle Him in Mine house and in My kingdom for ever; and His throne shall be established for ever more.

This was the coming Kingdom to which the Lord referred when He taught His disciples to pray, "Thy kingdom come,

1. Gen. 12:3; 17:19; 27:33; 49:8-11; 2 Sam. 7:8-16; Luke 1:32,33; 1 Chron. 17:11,14; 22:10; Gen. 13:14,15; 15:17,18; Rom. 11:29; Deut. 28:1,13; Acts 15:14-17; Luke 21:24; 1 Thess. 4; Zech. 12:9,10; Deut. 27:1-3,8-10; 2 Cor. 3:15,16; Ezek. 34:11-15; 37:21-28; Jer. 31:31-45; 32:37-40; Isa. 59: 20,21; 60:3,9-12; 61:3-6; 62:2-4; Jer. 30:18; Matt. 10:5-7; 15:24; 27:25; John 1:11

Thy will be done in earth, as it is in heaven." It is the "end time" to which Peter refers, "But the end of all things is at hand." Paul had it in mind when he wrote to Titus,

> Looking for that blessed hope, and the glorious appearing of the great God and our Saviour Jesus Christ.

James calls for patience in awaiting this coming kingdom:

> Be patient, therefore, brethren, unto the coming of the Lord . . . stablish your hearts: for the coming of the Lord draweth nigh.

However, by conquest Christ is to establish His theocratic kingdom of the Davidic dynasty, and this with force, as foretold in the second psalm:

> Ask of Me, and I shall give Thee [Christ] the heathen for Thine inheritance, and the uttermost parts of the earth for Thy possession. Thou shalt break them with a rod of iron: Thou shalt dash them in pieces like a potter's vessel.

The Psalmist also prophesied the golden age when Christ shall have supremacy over all creation, and the universal Christ-King shall reign over all nations of the earth:

> Lift up your heads, O ye gates; and be ye lifted up, ye everlasting doors; and the King of glory shall come in. Who is this King of glory? The Lord strong and mighty, the Lord mighty in battle.

Eight times in the New Testament the Psalmist is quoted as saying:

> The Lord said unto my Lord, sit Thou at My right hand, until I make Thine enemies Thy footstool.[2]

This is conquest over enemies by force when Christ comes.

The Psalmist also tells of the restoration of Israel under the spreading figure of a "vine," which is a type of Israel when

2. Psa. 2; Isa. 9:6,7; Psa. 8:1; 24:7,8; 89:35-37; 110:1,2

Shiloh (the peacemaker) shall come to be their king. The Psalmist declared that Christ is to have not only supremacy over all creation, "Who has set Thy glory above the heavens," but will have universal dominion:

> Thy throne, O God, is for ever and ever. . . .
> He that goeth forth and weepeth, bearing precious seed, shall doubtless come again with rejoicing, bringing His sheaves with Him.

This Sower is the Christ, the Son of man.[3]

Isaiah used the Hebrew word, *gibbor*, for prince, meaning "warrior"; hence the "Prince of Peace" is to be a "warrior hero," a militant Messiah. Isaiah prophesies that this King-Immanuel shall be called

> Wonderful, Counsellor, The mighty God, The everlasting Father, The Prince of Peace . . . upon the throne of David, and upon His kingdom, to order it, and establish it with judgment and with justice.

Isaiah gives the last and glorious invitation to the nations of earth to prepare for this golden age:

> And it shall come to pass in the latter days, that the mountain of Jehovah's house shall be established on the top of the mountains, and shall be exalted above the hills [little kingdom]; and all nations shall flow unto it. And many peoples shall go and say, Come ye, and let us go up to the mountain [kingdom] of Jehovah . . . for out of Zion shall go forth the law, and the word of Jehovah from Jerusalem.

"Mountain" in this scripture is a symbol of kingdom.

Jehovah makes a new covenant of kingship with David. He declares Himself as King:

> And thine house and thy kingdom shall be established for ever, before thee thy throne shall be established for ever.

3. Psa. 80:8; 45:6; 126:5,6

This covenant awaits fulfilment. The Christ-King as the Son of David is to reign and rule forever. Hence, His Second Advent is the hope of Israel and the nations.

> Of the increase of His government and peace there shall be no end, upon the throne of David . . . to establish it with judgment . . . from henceforth even for ever.

The Old Testament prophets give many beautiful types of this future golden age. Isaiah shows that God is providing a "shade," a "refuge," and a "pavilion" for those that are purified and separated unto Himself for His glorious reign. "Refuge" is a symbol of rest, peace, and safety that can only come to the nations of earth in that Sabbath-rest of the golden age.[4]

Jeremiah pictured the reunion of the people of the Lord:

> They shall call Jerusalem the throne of Jehovah . . . the house of Judah shall walk with the house of Israel.

Then, and not until then, will there be a "universal brotherhood of man" and a "universal fatherhood of God" on the earth. This can never be accomplished as long as there is greed, avarice, and hatred in the hearts of men, and the Saviour of men rejected.[5]

Ezekiel prophesied the restoration of Israel to her lands, and the Davidic kingdom to be set up:

> I will set up ONE Shepherd over them, and He shall feed them, even My servant David . . . and I the Lord will be their God, and My servant David a Prince among them; I the Lord have spoken it.[6]

Daniel foretold the golden age and the universal kingdom when Jehovah will rule and reign in peace and righteousness during the final world-empire:

4. Isa. 11:10; 25:4; 35:6-10; 66:1; Deut. 33:27; Gen. 14:3; Isa. 2:2,3
5. Jer. 3:17,18; S. of S. 2:8; Rev. 22:20
6. Ezek. 34:23,24

And in the day of these kings shall the God of heaven set up a kingdom, which shall never be destroyed.[7]

Hosea told of the unchanging love of Christ, the divine Lover, and likened Him unto the love Hosea still retained for his adulterous wife. Chastisement was necessary because of her apostasy. Here Israel is the prodigal child of God. "Whom the Lord loveth He chasteneth." Hosea stated that Israel shall finally seek her King-David, the Royal-Messiah, and find Him:

Afterward shall the children of Israel return, and seek the Lord their God, and David their king; and shall fear the Lord and His goodness in the latter days.

Hosea also described the ultimate blessings of Israel in the golden age when she shall have accepted her faithful Messiah.[8]

Joel tells of the Messianic salvation in the coming of the Spirit at Pentecost, to be fulfilled in a greater measure when Christ establishes His kingdom on the earth.[9]

Amos predicted the glorious golden age when the Lord shall return to re-establish the Davidic monarchy:

In that day will I raise up the tabernacle of David that is fallen, and close up the breaches thereof; and I will raise up his ruins, and I will build it as in the days of old.[10]

How perfectly these words agree with the prophecy quoted by James in Acts:

After this I will return, and will build again the tabernacle of David, which is fallen down; and I will build again the ruins thereof, and I will set it up.

7. Dan. 2:44; Heb. 12:6
8. Hosea 3:5
9. Joel 2:28-31; Acts 2:17; Heb. 1:1,2
10. Amos 9:11; Acts 15:15-17

Micah prophesied the First Coming of Christ and His birth, and also tells of a future time when the Christ-King shall come to establish His universal kingdom with its security and prosperity:

> And He shall judge among many people, and rebuke strong nations afar off; and they shall beat their swords into plowshares, and their spears into pruninghooks; nation shall not lift up a sword against nation, neither shall they learn war any more.[11]

Habakkuk proclaimed the advent of the golden age and the personal coming of the King-Jehovah with joy, confidence, and redemption of His people. This he shows will fully come when Christ, David's righteous Branch, shall set up His universal kingdom:

> For the earth shall be filled with the knowledge of the glory of the Lord, as the waters cover the sea.[12]

Zephaniah: The last words of this prophet give promise of the golden age and the joy in the restoration of the chosen people, and the perfect security of the redeemed, with their Redeemer-Christ:

> Sing, O daughter of Zion; shout, O Israel; be glad and rejoice with all the heart, O daughter of Jerusalem . . . even the Lord, is in the midst of thee: thou shalt not see evil any more.[13]

This golden age is of universal belief in some form to be realized at some time. It is the "Day of the Lord." At that time the *state* of the saints will be that of Christ after the resurrection.

Should we not pray with Milton: "Come forth out of Thy royal chambers, O Prince of all the kings of the earth! Put

11. Micah 4:1-3; 5:2
12. Hab. 2:14
13. Zeph. 3:14,15

on the visible robes of Thine imperial majesty, take up that unlimited sceptre which Thy Almighty Father hath bequeathed Thee; for now the voice of the bride calls Thee, and all creatures sigh to be renewed."

Chapter 20

CHRIST
and Israel

CENTURIES AFTER THE FLOOD, OLD TES-tament prophecy was confined to one nation—Israel—chosen of God to be a holy nation and a kingdom of priests. To this nation were the sufferings and glory of Jehovah to be revealed. Israel was an elect nation from the seed of Abraham. Later the Gentiles were to be made fellow heirs of his promise in Christ. When the promised Messiah appeared, He came to this elect nation. "Jesus Christ was a minister of the circumcision." He came to "the Jew first." Israel was to practise faith, the law of life. To fail in faith was to fail in life. As the Messiah, Christ made His primary appeal to Israel who longed for her Messiah-King. God has not forgotten His ancient people. His redemptive purposes center in Israel. "Salvation is of the Jews."

The Old Testament, as well as the New, is essentially a supernatural book. It can be best proved by the fulfilment of prophecy. Supernaturalism is not superstition. One is of God, the other of man. The ancient people of Egypt, Greece, and Babylon gave to the world superstition, pantheism, theosophy, and evolution, as well as spiritism and spiritualism. Only God could utter prophecy and history which would be fulfilled hundreds of years after. No prophecy is known among the writings of ancient philosophers, but is found only in the revelation of God in His Word.

El'Shaddai made a covenant with Abraham which was

unconditional. A covenant is an agreement, signed, sealed, and witnessed. Once ratified it could not be broken by any act of Abraham and certainly not of God. This Abrahamic covenant was signed by the covenant-keeping God, and sealed in the blood of the covenant, when Abraham was commanded to take the sacrificial animals and part them asunder.

This was called the *berith*, which meant covenant. The witness was in the circumcision, which was later changed under the New Covenant to an inward sign, a circumcised heart in the fulfilment of the law of the Lord. Failure on the part of Abraham's seed did not disannul this unconditional covenant. The Abrahamic seed was to be a royal, kingly line, coming from one common father, Abraham. The covenant made regarding the "seed" was wholly unconditional. This promise of Jehovah was irrespective of the moral or spiritual character of Abraham's posterity. In the covenant, God assumed all responsibility for its fulfilment. It stands on the integrity of God.

> By Myself have I sworn.
> Thy seed shall possess the gate of his enemies.
> In thy seed shall all the nations of the earth be blessed.

This is the Messianic promise. Paul said, "Now to Abraham and his seed were the promises made . . . And to thy seed, which is Christ."

> And this I say, that the covenant, that was confirmed before of God in Christ, the law, which was four hundred and thirty years after, cannot disannul that it should make the promise of none effect.

In the twelfth chapter of Genesis are found the following covenants made to Abraham, Isaac, and Jacob: to make Abraham a great nation; to make his name great; to bless those that bless him; to curse those that curse him; in him the families of earth would be blessed; a nation from which kings shall come; Israel's dispersion foretold; and the preservation and restoration of His people.

God's eternal purpose of Christ includes the Jew. He is the fulfilment of the Messianic hope of Israel. God's promise to Abraham was, "In thee shall all the families of the earth be blessed." This was partially fulfilled in giving to the world a Saviour, born of a Jewess. It will be entirely fulfilled in the coming of Israel's Messiah at His Second Advent.[1]

"The mystery [divine secret] of Israel" referred to in Romans is now being revealed:

> I would not, brethren, that ye should be ignorant of this mystery . . . that blindness in part is happened to Israel, until the fulness of the Gentiles be come in. And so all Israel shall be saved; as it is written, There shall come out of Zion the Deliverer, and shall turn away ungodliness from Jacob.

This Deliverer is Christ. In the ninth chapter of Romans Paul expressed his grief at Israel's rejection of Christ. In the tenth chapter he described Israel's refusing salvation through faith in Christ, and her trying to justify herself by the works of the flesh. In chapter eleven we have Israel ultimately returning to God, with only a remnant of true believers having been saved by grace and incorporated in the church. Israel failed as a theocratic nation. God did not fail Israel.

"The mystery of Israel" consists of her partial blindness throughout past ages because of unbelief. Salvation came to the Gentiles because of Israel's fall. However, Israel's national restoration is promised in Christ's kingdom to come, and with the acceptance of her Messiah.

1. Rom. 1:16; 9:4,5; John 4:22; Gen. 15; 17:1-8; Deut. 30:6; Jer. 31; Ezek. 36:24; Heb. 8; Gal. 3:16,17; 1 Pet. 1:25; Ezek. 37:14; Gen. 22:16-18; Lev. 26:33-45; Rom. 11

Ezekiel said:

> I will take you from among the heathen, and gather you
> out of all countries, and will bring you into your own
> land.

Paul showed that the wild olive (typical of the Gentiles)
is being grafted into the true olive (the Jew) and that there
is neither Jew nor Gentile in God's plan of redemption.
Israel fell by unbelief, but the Gentile was grafted in by
faith. In these latter days there is a "remnant according to
the election of grace" from the Jewish nation which will
be saved, among whom the Apostle Paul and others are
included. All such are saved by grace through faith in the
Lord Jesus Christ. During this partial blindness of Israel,
the bride, as the body of Christ, is being completed for
her Bridegroom.

God's covenant with Sarah was inflexible and His word
to Abraham insurmountable:

> Sarah thy wife shall bear thee a son indeed; and thou
> shalt call his name Isaac; and I . . . will multiply him
> exceedingly.

Isaac was to be the *legal* line whose posterity are "the
children of promise." Only the children of Isaac are to be
counted for the legal seed of the covenant and the recipients
of national promise of honor, glories, adoption, covenants,
special service, and those through whom Christ came.

The other posterity of Abraham and Isaac are the
"children of the flesh." God declares Himself as being the
"God of Abraham, Isaac, and Jacob," rather than the God
of Abraham, Ishmael, and Esau. This is an "election of *race*
rather than of *grace*."

God will use Israel to vindicate His Word and His Son-
Christ among the nations of the earth, that all may know

"That I Am He." [2] The hope of Israel is in Christ. Paul declared that the unbelief of Israel as a nation is only "until the fulness of the Gentiles be come in."

Scripture cannot be understood apart from the history of Israel. Some would regard the crucifixion of Jesus as disproving His claim to royalty and kingship. They overlook the fact that over 700 years before His birth Isaiah had prophesied:

> When we shall see Him, there is no beauty that we should desire Him: He is despised and rejected of men; a man of sorrows, and acquainted with grief; and we hid as it were our faces from Him; He was despised, and we esteemed Him not.

Had Israel accepted the Messiah-Christ in His humiliation it would have been a strong argument against Christianity, and would have proved that the Scriptures were false. It was prophesied that He would be rejected and crucified. It is clear that Israel was to reject her Messiah "until the fulness of the Gentiles be come in."

Ezekiel tells of Israel's unification under one King in the days to come:

> I will take the children of Israel . . . and I will make them one nation . . . upon the mountains of Israel; and one King shall be King to them all.

Christ is Israel's national hope and expectation. This is also taught in Ezekiel's story of the "valley of dry bones":

> These bones are the whole house of Israel . . . ye shall live, and I shall place you in your own land.

Deuteronomy 28 gives a prophecy of the ills that would overtake Israel for not obeying God. However, just as truly

2. Jer. 31:10,11; Rom. 11; Rom. 9:11-14; Acts 15:14-16; Hosea 13:9; 14:1; Isa. 43:1,10-12; 53:2,3; Psa. 118:22; Isa. 6:9-12; Ezek. 36:24-38; 37:11; Deut. 28:37,65,66; Zech. 2:12

will the prophecies be fulfilled relative to their return as a nation to the land as rightful owners.

The Old Testament reveals God in history, culminating in the Day of Jehovah. This was the Messianic hope of Israel, the coming of their Messiah. The New Testament reveals that Israel's Messiah came in the Person of Jesus, but His birth did not usher in the Day of Jehovah. The Anointed One introduced the kingdom of heaven. Being rejected the king is now in heaven, and His subjects on earth are awaiting the Day of Jehovah.

A comparison has been given between the Jew and Christ:

THE JEW	CHRIST
Has peculiar God-given characteristics.	Conceived of God, differs from all others.
Has been burned, persecuted, torn asunder.	Has been beaten, bruised, persecuted, crucified.
Has been wilfully misunderstood.	Has been wilfully misquoted and misunderstood.
Cannot be ignored by the world.	Condemned, but cannot be ignored by the world.
Finds himself in fulfilled prophecy.	Proves Himself in fulfilled prophecy.
Cursed and unwanted in every land.	Rejected and hated in every land.
As a race can never be destroyed.	The eternal, can never be destroyed.
Hated by other religionists.	Hated by all except Christians.
Has seen the rise and fall of other nations.	Will rule and reign over every nation.
Claims to be the "chosen of God" for salvation.	Chooses both Jew and Gentile for salvation.
Scattered to the four corners of the earth.	To be heralded in all nations of the earth.
Increased in numbers under persecution.	Has increased under assaults of His enemies.
Leaves his mark wherever he goes.	Quoted more than all living men of all ages.

THE JEW	CHRIST
At home with the rich and the poor.	Made His home with the rich and the poor.
Reaches life at every point.	Exerts His influence in every phase of life.
"Shall not be reckoned among the nations."	Stands alone, not to be reckoned as others.
Has been neglected by the Gentiles.	Has been neglected by the Jews.
Proves the inspiration of the Bible.	Gives illumination to the Bible.
Will be gathered to her promised land.	Foretells the restoration to the promised land.
Accused of causing strife and bloodshed.	Accused of causing division and discord.

While God called out from the nations the people of Israel to be in a special way His own, the fact remains that He never ceased to be the God of all nations. This is affirmed in the words of Paul to the Romans:

Is He the God of the Jews only? is He not also of the Gentiles? Yea, of the Gentiles also.

Chapter 21

CHRIST
the "Branch"

THE MESSIAH-CHRIST IS PRESENTED IN the Old Testament prophets as THE BRANCH.[1]

Behold, the days come, saith the Lord, that I will raise unto David a righteous Branch, and a King shall reign and prosper, and shall execute judgment and justice in the earth.

Behold, I will bring forth My servant The Branch.
Behold, the man, whose name is The Branch.
In that day shall The Branch of the Lord be beautiful and glorious.

These Messianic prophecies of THE BRANCH fit perfectly the four Gospels:[2]

Matthew, showing Christ as King of the Jews, revealing the Messiah's kingship, as foretold by the prophets. "Behold, thy King cometh unto thee."

Mark, showing Christ as Servant of Jehovah, with the key-word "go"—going about serving. "Behold My servant, whom I uphold."

Luke, showing Christ as man, Son of Man, in His humanity, seeking the lost. "Behold, the man, whose name is The Branch."

John, showing Christ in His Deity, Son of God, the only begotten of the Father. "Behold, your God."

1. Jer. 23:5; 33:15; Isa. 4:2; 11:1; Zech. 3:8; 6:12; John 15:1,2
2. Zech. 9:9; 6:12; Isa. 42:1; 40:9; Phil. 2:6,8; John 3:13; 5:18; 8:58; 10:30

The word LORD is not mentioned in Mark's Gospel until after the Resurrection. It presents the Lord as Jehovah's Servant. The servant is not usually addressed as "Lord," which shows the perfect accuracy of the Scriptures. Neither is there any genealogy of Jesus recorded in Mark's Gospel.

JESUS (Greek) is the same as JOSHUA (Hebrew) meaning "Salvation of Jehovah," or "Jehovah-Saviour," and appears 85 times in Mark's Gospel. The name JESUS expresses relationship of Jehovah in incarnation, and the shame endured in saving His people from their sins.

The Tabernacle in Exodus gives a type anticipating the four Gospels.[3] The veil is in four colors: blue, purple, scarlet, white, "with cherubim" hung upon four pillars of wood overlaid with gold . . . and sockets of silver. Blue, symbolizing eternity, the heavenliness of Christ; Purple, the royalty and kingliness of Christ; Scarlet, the Cross, and sufferings of Christ; White, the purity, sinlessness, and holiness of Christ; Gold, symbolizing the Deity and sovereignty of Christ; Silver, the redemption and sacrifice of Christ; Wood, the incarnation and humanity of Christ, "His flesh"; Pillars, being four, display the beauty of the veil.

Here the four Gospels display the beauty of the Person and work of Christ. The veil of the Tabernacle was ornamented with cherubim with four faces. The four cherubim are described in Ezekiel as "living creatures," which identifies the four living creatures in the Revelation, and with the Lord Jesus Christ in the four Gospels. The cherubim seem to be a celestial order of spirit-beings, distinguished from ordinary angels who are simply messengers. They seem to be connected with the throne of God and appear to be ministers of the Deity, often associated with judgments. Above the blood-sprinkled mercy-seat in the most holy place the cherubim appear to be connected with the atone-

3. Ex. 26:31,32; Heb. 10:19,20

ment of Christ, and are embroidered on the veil as representing incarnation and redemption.

The cherubim of Ezekiel are represented by four symbolic heads of animate creation; the lion, calf, man, and eagle:[4]

Lion, the king of beasts, portraying Christ as King. Here the cherubim pictures Christ in the Gospel of Matthew as the "Son of David, the King of the Jews."

Calf (young ox). This was the animal for patience, sacrifice, and service. This second cherubim pictures Christ as "The servant of Jehovah," as seen in the Gospel of Mark.

Man; the third cherubim shows "The son of man," corresponding with the Gospel of Luke, displaying the humanity of Christ.

Eagle is the one that soars above the earth in the heavenlies. This fourth cherubim is portraying the Deity of Christ, the Son of God, as shown in the Gospel of John. Here Christ is the great "I AM."

The genealogy of Christ goes back to Adam because Luke shows Christ as the "Son of man," including *all* mankind. In Luke's Gospel Christ is showing His self-dependence upon the Father, as indicated by His prayers. His human sympathy is also shown in His weeping, healing, and in Gethsemane.

The word "Branch" is also a type of the believers' union with Christ, and the prosperity that awaits the righteous. A prophetic picture of THE BRANCH shows the glory of the golden age that is to follow this present dispensation:

And there shall come forth a rod out of the stem of Jesse, and a Branch shall grow out of his roots.

This prophecy of THE BRANCH also refers to the Davidic covenant of the glorious kingdom of Christ, "The seed of David according to the flesh."

4. Ezek. 10:14-17; Rev. 4:7; 5:5; Jer. 33:15

In those days, and at that time, will I cause the Branch of righteousness to grow up unto David; and He shall execute judgment and righteousness in the land.

Jeremiah tells of the victories of THE BRANCH. The "branch" (lowly sprout, the thing despised) shall have dominion as the King of the Jews. By some the King today is despised and rejected; but by others the gold, frankincense, and myrrh are to be laid at His feet. Some are still saying, "Can any good thing come out of Nazareth?" while others are crowning Him "King of kings and Lord of lords." He fulfilled the prophecies of shame, as He will some day the predictions of glory.

Chapter 22

CHRIST
the "Rock"

THE *ROCK* IS USED MANY TIMES IN THE Old Testament as a type of Christ, and is confirmed by the Apostle Paul in the New:

> And did all drink the same spiritual drink: for they drank of that spiritual Rock that followed them; and that Rock was Christ.

Moses sang typically of that ROCK:

> He is the Rock, His work is perfect . . .
> He made him [Jacob] to suck honey out of the Rock;
> But Jeshurun [Israel] . . . forsook God . . . and lightly esteemed the Rock of his salvation.
>
> Of the Rock that begat thee thou art unmindful, and hast forgotten God that formed thee.
> How should one chase a thousand, and two put ten thousand to flight, except their Rock had sold them. . . .

This water-giving ROCK was typical of Christ, who is the water and well of life.[1]

Moses led the children of Israel in the wilderness of Mt. Horeb. They were in need of water, and there was none at Rephidim. The people chided Moses. Going to the right source of relief, Moses prayed to God, "What shall I do unto this people?" God answered, "Thou shalt smite the rock, and there shall come water out of it."

1. Deut. 32:4,13,15,18,30; 1 Cor. 10:4

God shows His grace to a rebellious people. Water is a type here of the grace of God, and the "free water" of free salvation amid unmerited favor. The smiting of the rock was a real act performed by a living person, which brought forth physical water. Tradition says the water, in cool springs, followed the children of Israel in the desert as a providential act of Jehovah. Only this could sustain long such a large company. That is why they did not die of thirst.

The children of Israel were again in need of water, and God commanded Moses to "speak ye unto the rock." Instead Moses "smote the rock" the second time. God said to Moses, "Because ye believed Me not, . . . therefore ye shall not bring this congregation into the land which I have given them." Typically, the Rock-Christ was to be smitten but *once*, and for all time. On the Cross Christ finished His work of redemption which needs no repeating. This, in type, was denied by Moses. His disobedience kept him out of Canaan.[2]

Moses shows that Christ is the ROCK of perfection: "He is the rock, His work is perfect." The believer finds his perfection, righteousness, and sanctification in the perfection of the Rock-Christ. It is the smitten ROCK on the Cross that God accepts: "A broken and a contrite heart" brings the "water of life" to a thirsty world. Someone has said: The broken strength of Jacob brought spiritual power; the broken pitchers of Gideon's 300 brought victory; the broken etiquette of Esther brought deliverance; the broken loaves of Jesus fed the five thousand; the broken alabaster box of Mary exhibited her love; the broken body of Jesus on the Cross brought salvation; the broken hearts today find healing

2. Ex. 17:2-6; Num. 20:8-11; Deut. 8:15; Psa. 78:15,16,20; John 4:10,14; 7:37-39; Rom. 5:19; Rev. 22:17

in the Rock-Christ. Jacob took a stone for a pillow and lay down to rest after leaving Beersheba.[3]

The Psalmist rejoiced in the assurance of the believers' preservation in the Christ-Rock; "The Lord is my rock, and my fortress, and my deliverer." David showed the grace of Christ in providing blessings and salvation for the needy: "He opened the rock and the waters gushed out; they ran in the dry places like a river."

The Psalmist also shows the sweetness of salvation: "With honey out of the rock should I have satisfied thee." He also cried:

> The Lord is my Rock, and my fortress, and my deliverer.
> Unto thee will I cry, O Lord my Rock.
> I will say unto God my Rock.
> Lead me to the Rock that is higher than I.
> He only is my Rock and my salvation.
> The Rock of Israel spake to me.
> God of my Rock; in Him will I trust.

And again the Psalmist sang joyfully:

> O come, let us sing unto Jehovah; let us make a joyful noise to the Rock of our salvation. Let us come before His presence with thanksgiving; let us make a joyful noise unto Him with psalms. For Jehovah is a great God, And a great King above all gods . . . O come, let us worship and bow down; let us kneel before Jehovah our Maker.

Jehovah was Israel's Rock in suffering and need, and they continued to sing:

> And they remembered that God was their Rock, and the Most High God their Redeemer.

Isaiah would use the Rock as a hiding place, and a covert from the tempests of life:

3. Ex. 33:22; Isa. 55:1; 12:3; 32:2; 2 Sam. 22:2,3; 23:3; Eph. 2:20

As rivers of water in a dry place, as the shadow of a great rock in a weary land.

Isaiah also shows, in type, that Christ is the ROCK, and each believer a chip off the ROCK: "Look unto the Rock whence ye are hewn." Also, the "Rock of offence" to the unbelieving: "But for a stone of stumbling and for a rock of offence." [4]

Judges records the "Fire out of the Rock." God speaking to Gideon says:

Surely I will be with thee, and thou shalt smite the Midianites . . . Take the flesh and the unleavened cakes, and lay them upon this rock . . . and there rose up fire out of the rock, and consumed the flesh and the unleavened cakes.

This is the ROCK in judgment upon Israel's apostasy as well as upon her enemies. Fire blesses and blights, heals and hurts, purifies and destroys.

Samuel looked to that ROCK for help:

Then Samuel took a stone, and set it between Mizpeh and Shen, and called the name of it Ebenezer, saying, Hitherto hath the Lord helped us.

To the Gentile nations the Christ-Rock is a stone "cut out without hands"; to the Jew Christ's first coming was "a stumbling block, a Rock of offence"; to the unbeliever the Christ-Rock will be "a crushing stone" in judgment; to the church a "chief corner Stone."

The ROCK of Judgment shall be the fate of the one who rejects the "Smitten Rock" of Calvary:

And whosoever shall fall on this stone shall be broken; but on whomsoever it shall fall, it will grind him to powder.

4. Psa. 18:2,31; 28:1; 42:9; 61:2; 62:2,6,7; 94:22; 95:1; 105:41; 81:16

The Rock is either for salvation or condemnation; weal or woe; heaven or hell. The Rock ("smitten stone") shall some day come from heaven, destroying the then existing world empires, after which the Rock will fill the earth with His glory. From that storm comes the calm of the promised golden age:

> Thou sawest till that a stone was cut out without hands, which smote the image . . . and brake them to pieces.

Jesus would use the Rock (Greek, *petra*) as a foundation for His church, saying:

> Upon this rock I will build My church; and the gates of hell shall not prevail against it.

In the Septuagint *petra* is used one hundred and four times, meaning a "great rock," such as the great rocks of Horeb.[5]

5. Judges 6:16-21; 1 Sam. 7:12; Isa. 8:14,15; 2 Sam. 23:3; Dan. 2:31-35; Matt. 21:44; 1 Pet. 2:8; Rom. 9:32,33; 1 Cor. 1:23; Deut. 11:26-29; Matt. 16:18

Chapter 23

CHRIST
and Virgin Birth

THE DOCTRINES OF FINAL AUTHORITY OF the Bible are the atoning death of Jesus, His bodily resurrection, the lordship and intercession of Christ, and His second advent. These depend upon the virgin birth of Christ. Also, Christ had to become man in order to manifest God to man.

"Virgin" (Hebrew, *almah*) means a lass, damsel, maiden; not *bethoolah*, a young woman. It was used for Rebekah, the virgin bride of Isaac. Christ never spoke of Mary as His mother, but "woman." Mary simply *bore* the Son of man: "But a body hast thou prepared Me." The virgin had no right to David's throne, but Joseph did, as a descendant of David. Through Joseph, the legal foster father, Christ secured His right to be "King of the Jews."

With the destruction of the Temple in A.D. 70 by Titus, all records of the genealogies of the twelve tribes of Israel were lost. Today no Jew can prove from which tribe he came. The tribal records would have shown plainly that Christ was a descendant of King David and entitled to the throne.

Prophecies of the virgin birth of Christ were given hundreds of years before Jesus was born. It was prophesied that the "seed" of Abraham was to become the heir of the "promised land." God said to Abraham:

I will give unto thee, and to thy seed after thee, the land wherein thou art a stranger, all the land of Canaan, for an everlasting possession.

Paul confirmed this prophecy:

> Now to Abraham and his seed were the promises made.
> He saith not, And to seeds, as of many; but as of one,
> And to thy seed, which is Christ.

Christ was to be the "Seed of the woman," not of man.
Science says there is no such thing as the "seed of the
woman"; the "seed" is masculine and life is from the male.
The birth of Christ was a biological miracle. Christ had no
earthly father. As was the custom, He took His name from
his legal father, Joseph.

Courtship in the days of Abraham was interesting. The
family of the intended groom did the proposing, and a friend
sent to make it known. If agreeable, the contract was consummated with gifts. After a year had elapsed, the virgin,
with her chaperone, was brought to the friend who com-
municated with the bridegroom, and the couple were considered married. Before Joseph and Mary had come together
in marriage relationship, they were considered married.[1]

The Gospel of Matthew records the royal line, the *regal*
rights of Christ to the throne, from Abraham through David;
getting the land through the Abrahamic covenant, and getting the throne through the Davidic covenant.

The Gospel of Luke records the royal line, the *legal*
right, from Adam through Abraham, David, Nathan, and
Mary.

The Gospel of John gives no genealogy but states, "And
the Word was made flesh, and dwelt among us."

Moses in the Pentateuch bore his unequivocal testimony
to the virgin birth of Christ by showing that the "seed
of the woman" would bruise the serpent's head; that Shiloh
would come to gather back His people; that the Star out
of Jacob, and the Sceptre shall arise out of Israel; that they
would harken to the great Prophet whom God should raise

1. Gen. 17:8; Gal. 3:16

up; and that the serpent in the wilderness should be raised up, which Christ interpreted as prophetic of Himself. To make this prophecy doubly sure Christ added, "Moses wrote of Me." [2]

Moses in the law required a threefold testimony of witnesses: "At the mouth of three witnesses, shall the matter be established." Paul said, "In the mouth of two or three witnesses shall every word be established." We have a threefold witness of the virgin birth of Christ in Gabriel, the angel sent of the Lord with the annunciation; the Wise Men coming to worship Him as King; and Pilate, saying, "Art thou a king then?" Jesus answered, "To this end was I born."

God adds His own testimony through the Psalmist, saying, "I will make Him My first-born, higher than the kings of the earth." This refers to the Emmanuel-King, looking beyond the Davidic covenant to One higher than the kings of earth. This prophecy is referred to by the writer of the Hebrews:

When he bringeth in the first-begotten into the world, he saith, And let all the angels of God worship Him.

When Christ came into the world as virgin-born Son of God the angels shouted, "Glory to God in the highest, and on earth peace, good will toward men." When Christ comes the second time, as the first-born from among the dead, He will be praised by men and angels.[3]

Among the prophecies of the Old Testament that have found their fulfilment in the New, relative to the birth of Jesus, are:

But thou, Bethlehem Ephrathah, though thou be little among the thousands of Judah, yet out of thee shall He come forth unto Me that is to be ruler in Israel.

2. Gen. 3:15; John 1:14; Num. 24:17; 21:9; John 3:14,15; Deut. 18:18; Luke 24:44; John 5:46
3. Num. 35:30; Deut. 17:6; 19:15; Matt. 18:16; John 8:17; Heb. 10:28; Psa. 89:27; Heb. 1:2,6

Micah speaks with authority in foretelling the coming of the King. No one would have expected a ruler or king to come from little Bethlehem.

Hosea prophesied, I "called my Son out of Egypt."

This statement of Hosea not only had a historic but also a prophetic value. Primarily, it refers to Israel as a nation, calling her out of spiritual harlotry and pollution, and the receiving of her chastisement, but calling her back to her first love, Jehovah. After four hundred years a "child" is born, and Matthew's Gospel uses the love quotation of Hosea to his estranged wife as applying to Christ. The history of Hosea saw the child (Israel) going into Egypt, but it is also a type, as Matthew sees it, of the child-Christ coming out of Egypt. While Matthew's Gospel might well be called the "Gospel of rejection" it can also be called the "good tidings of deliverance."

Jeremiah records:

> A voice was heard in Ramah, lamentation, and bitter weeping; Rachel weeping for her children refused to be comforted for her children, because they were not. Thus saith the Lord; Refrain thy voice from weeping, and thine eyes from tears; for thy work shall be rewarded, saith the Lord.

And Isaiah says, "And there shall come forth a rod out of the stem of Jesse, and a Branch shall grow out of his roots."

In this prophecy Jeremiah tells the doom of a dying nation, and Rachel lamenting the destruction of her descendants. Her anguish found a counterpart in the grief of the mothers in Bethlehem. The prophet gives a ray of hope and comfort in the coming of a Deliverer-Christ. The Gospel of Matthew quotes this prophecy but only that portion dealing with the doom and weeping. Rachel's weeping is to cease, for the King has come.[4]

4. Micah 5:2; Hosea 11:1; Jer. 31:15-18; 33:15; Isa. 11:1

The Old Testament closes looking for the coming of the Messiah, which was prophesied 398 years before fulfilment:

Behold, I will send My messenger, and he shall prepare the way before Me; and the Lord, whom ye seek, shall suddenly come to His temple.

Malachi saw both Advents of Christ, but did not separate them in his prophecy.

Isaiah gives the prophecy of the Immanuel, the virgin's son:

Behold, a [the] virgin shall conceive, and bear a son, and shall call His name Immanuel.

The definite article is here used. Not "a" but *the* virgin. The prophet blazes out into greater splendor:

For unto us a child is born, unto us a son is given; and the government shall be upon His shoulder; and His name shall be called Wonderful, Counsellor, The mighty God, The everlasting Father, The Prince of Peace.

The ultimate fulfilment of this prophecy is found in the angelic promise of the virgin birth:

She shall bring forth a son, and thou shalt call His name JESUS: for He shall save His people from their sins.

This was the first prophecy fulfilled in the New Testament.[5]

The "Son of man" has been promised dominion over the earth. The "first Adam" lost it, the "last Adam" regained it.

Let us make man . . . have dominion . . . upon the earth.

The Paradise lost by Adam will be more than regained in Christ:

5. Mal. 3:1-6; Matt. 11:10; Mark 1:2; Luke 7:27; Isa. 7:14; 9:6; Matt. 1:21; Luke 1:31

> Thou madest Him to have dominion over the works of Thy hands; Thou hast put all things under His feet . . . O Lord our Lord, how excellent is Thy name in all the earth!

Truly the Son of God is heir to all things, and will some day possess them:

> Hath in these last days spoken unto us by His Son, whom He hath appointed heir of all things, by whom He also made the worlds.

The birth of Christ is promised as the "Star," a type of Christ who was to rise and guide His people:

> I shall see Him, but not now: I shall behold Him, but not nigh: there shall come a Star out of Jacob, and a Sceptre shall rise out of Israel.

Sceptre (Hebrew, *shevet*) is a symbol of the sovereignty of Christ, indicating His holy character and righteous acts in judgment:

> The Sceptre shall not depart from Judah, nor a lawgiver from between his feet, until Shiloh come; and unto Him shall the gathering of the people be.

Shiloh (Hebrew, *melech*, meaning King; *Hammashiach*, Messiah) is a name given to Christ, the word meaning "The Peace-maker." This prophecy has a twofold reference, to both Christ's First and Second Coming. It is plainly shown in the seven "shalls" of the Gospel of Luke:

> And, behold, thou *shalt* conceive in thy womb, and bring forth a son, and *shalt* call His name Jesus. He *shall* be great, and *shall* be called the Son of the Highest: and the Lord God *shall* give unto Him the throne of His father David; And He *shall* reign over the house of Jacob for ever: and of His kingdom there *shall* be no end.

The first four "shalls" have been literally carried out, and the last three are awaiting fulfilment at the Second Advent of Christ.

Isaiah prophesied that this virgin-born child should be called "Wonderful" (Hebrew "*peleh*"). Here the Hebrew word has even a deeper meaning—that of "miraculous, mysterious, indescribable, unfathomable," which only could apply to Deity. Only Christ could say, "Search the Scriptures [O.T.] . . . they are they which testify of Me."

The birth of Jesus was miraculous in that never was a man born like Him. The word "miracle" finds its fulfilment in the birth of Christ. Without this virgin-birth all prophecy would be meaningless. It was timed by God, "When the fulness of time was come, God sent forth His Son." A new chronology began at His birth. It was the center of time and history. Upon the birth of no other man has the world been so dependent.[6]

6. Gen. 1:26; Psa. 8:6,9; Heb. 1:2,6; Gen. 49:10; Num. 24:17; Luke 1:31-33; Gal. 4:4

Chapter 24

CHRIST
and Grace in the Old Testament

THE GOSPEL OF GRACE GIVEN TO THE nations was promised through the prophets of the Old Testament. Peter declared that the Old Testament prophets spoke of these present days of grace. Paul told Agrippa that he was preaching "nothing but what the prophets and Moses did say should come." John in the Revelation testified that "the testimony of Jesus is the spirit of prophecy." The Psalmist clearly foretold the dispensation of grace:

> Jehovah saith unto my Lord, Sit Thou at My right hand, until I make Thine enemies Thy footstool.

Here we see the two Advents of the one Messiah and the interval of grace between them.

The covenant of grace was made before man was created, or the foundations of the earth were laid; hence, the contracting parties, of necessity, were divine. Such was ineffectual without a vicarious sacrifice and a priest, essential features of the covenant of grace. God had designs of grace toward fallen humanity. He is still carrying out His will of purpose and design. Grace is seen in the Old Testament, "when the Spirit of God moved upon the face of the waters," and hope begins to dawn. Here divine activity begins, which was a prime necessity. The Spirit of God must "move" to produce a new creation and restoration.

God saves the sinner on the basis of His justice. He cannot

do wrong or condone sin. Christ met justice in His sacrifice, thus showing grace. The Just takes the place of the unjust. Justice calls for holiness, righteousness, and purity.

Every transgression must receive "a just recompense of reward." The full dimension of perfection is found only in the holiness of Christ. He alone could take the sinner's place. Righteousness must precede grace. The background of grace is a ruined race, from which the law demanded perfection. This Christ provided. Calvary saved the sinner from the penalty of sin. This is *grace*. Christ must lose His life to give it to others. He is the Giver of the life He demands. Salvation must come either by merit or grace. Grace provides it in the sacrifice of Christ, meeting the requirements of a just God.

Satan's philosophy of life is self-preservation; Christ's is propagation (life) by sacrifice. God's amazing grace is shown in the first two verses of the Bible. We read, "In the beginning God created . . ." Here is *generation* (creation). It must have been perfect, according to the nature of God.

Again we read, "The earth became void" or vain (Revised Version). Isaiah says, He "created it *not* in vain" (Hebrew, *void*). God's original creation of the earth was perfect. It must have become chaotic, perhaps from some great catastrophe caused by sin. This was *degeneration*.

We read again, "The Spirit of God moved," displaying His marvelous grace. This is *regeneration* (re-creation).

Grace is also seen in God's first promise in the Bible, the unconditional covenant made with Adam:

And I will put enmity between thee and the woman, and between thy seed and her seed: it shall bruise thy head, and thou shalt bruise his heel.

The judgment upon the serpent was God's first manifestation of grace to fallen man. This covenant will be completely fulfilled in the "Seed" who shall bruise the serpent's head. God's first promised judgment upon the serpent was in order that He might show His loving grace to Adam, and to all fallen, helpless creatures.[1]

The cherubim and the revolving sword of fire in Paradise seem to have been a covenant of hope to Adam. This was an earnest of the fact that some future day he and his posterity might have access to the Tree of Life. All this was because of the grace of God. The covenant of grace is shown as soon as sin begins. God calls, "Adam where art thou?" Here the picture of grace is seen in God seeking man, not man seeking God. "Come" is the invitation of grace.

After Cain slew Abel and no promised "seed" was forthcoming, the hope of Eve must have been turned to despondency. After 130 years of waiting she was rewarded. The covenant-keeping God gave her Seth from whom the promised "Seed" should come. The line of the Seth-Christ again shows the grace of God. Grace was offered Cain in the preservation of his life:

> Whosoever slayeth Cain, vengeance shall be taken on him sevenfold. And the Lord set a mark upon Cain, lest any finding him should kill him.

The covenant of grace was made with Noah because of his piety, and no conditions were required of his descendants. This was apparent in the rainbow given by God as a sign, and as declared by the prophet Isaiah. In the covenant with Noah, God said;

> This is the token of the covenant, which I have established between Me and all flesh that is upon the earth.

This covenant with Noah was made upon a sacrifice, and so was the unconditional covenant of grace. The inhabitants

---

1. 1 Pet. 1:10; 2 Pet. 1:2; Acts 26:22,23; Rev. 19:10; Psa. 110:1; Gen. 1:1-2; Isa. 45:18; Gen. 3:14,15

of earth met the flood of divine judgment, but Noah was safely shut in by God:

> And the Spirit of God moved upon the face of the waters.

Here is where sovereign grace intervenes. Earth could not resurrect itself. Ruined creation was helpless. God purposed in grace to bring forth a "new creation." Through the divine grace of God, Noah was saved and kept within the ark. Every nail driven in the ark was a call from sin and judgment unto salvation.[2]

Salvation by grace in the new covenant is not a contradiction of that in the old, but is its fulfilment, its completion. The Old Testament saints were saved by grace looking forward to the Cross. God accepted a substitute, a symbolic sacrifice. In the substitution of the animal, man died in his substitute.

God, in sovereign grace, called Abram to a life of separation, to whom He made great conditional as well as unconditional promises. Grace provided the covenant with Abram and his descendants:

> In that same day the Lord made a covenant with Abram, saying, Unto thy seed have I given this land, from the river of Egypt unto the great river, the river Euphrates.

God confirmed this covenant to Abram, saying, "I will make of thee a great nation." This was in Abram's natural posterity, as the "dust of the earth" through the Hebrew people. "Look now toward heaven, . . . so shall thy seed be." This last reference refers to Abram's spiritual posterity, whether Jew or Gentile. "I will bless thee," temporally and spiritually, and "make thy name great." This is universally true today regarding Abraham among Jews, Mohammedans, and Christians.

2. Matt. 11:28; Isa. 55:1-3; Gen. 3:7-15; 4:15; 9:17; Isa. 54:9,10

That the blessing of Abraham might come on the Gentiles through Jesus Christ; that we might receive the promise of the Spirit through faith.

The covenant of grace to Abram ends by saying, "In thee shall all the families of the earth be blest." This is being fulfilled in Christ. "Your father Abraham rejoiced to see My day," and Paul added, "And to thy seed, which is Christ."

This grace is shown to Abraham upon his leaving the appointed place of Jehovah and going into Egypt. In loving grace God protected the lives of Abraham and Sarah, who repented, were forgiven, and were given Isaac the promised son in their old age.

Ishmael, the son of the bondwoman, is the covenant given on Mount Sinai and represents the law. Such demands perfect obedience, even though sinful nature prevents it. Isaac is the covenant of grace in Christ, who, being perfect, has kept the law perfectly. The believer now has a higher law within him, the law of love. Ishmael represents the natural birth, which cannot inherit the kingdom of God; Isaac, the supernatural birth of the spirit of grace, bringing freedom from the bondage of the law.

Grace cannot be perverted, for it is of God. Those "in grace" have a perfection in Christ. He says, "I am in the Father, and ye [the believer] in Me, and I in you." Hence, Christ becomes to the saint wisdom, righteousness, sanctification, and redemption.[3]

The covenant of the grace of God is shown to Jacob (*supplanter*) who, although a crook, finally confessed that he was a Jacob. In grace, God changed his name to Israel, "A Prince." Later, by grace, Jacob and his family were preserved from famine in Canaan, Joseph being in Egypt by the permissive will of God.

3. Gen. 12:1-4; 15:18; Gal. 3:14; Gen. 22:16,17

Another instance of grace is seen in Naomi, whose Hebrew name was "Pleasant." She left God's country of Bethlehem-Judea ("house of bread") and went among the enemies of Israel and of God. She remained there ten years in her backslidden condition. Naomi was chastised of God three times; in the death of her husband, the marrying of her two sons to heathen girls, and finally in the death of her two sons. "But God" in His grace restored Naomi, who said in her bitterness, "Call me not Naomi, call me Mara [*bitter*]: for the Almighty hath dealt very bitterly with me." Later Ruth, the daughter-in-law of Naomi, became the ancestress of Christ.

The covenant of grace is beautifully seen in God's dealings with the children of Israel, conditioned upon repentance and faith. According to His elective love and grace He chose this people through whom the Redeemer was to come. In their journeyings they were down in Egypt forgetting God, semi-pagans and rebellious. "But God" in grace provided a deliverer in Moses. While the Israelites were wanderers in the wilderness of unbelief and defeat for forty years, Jehovah in grace finally brought them out. In grace He led them through the river Jordan and miraculously placed them in Canaan, a country of plenty, power, and privilege.

God in grace allowed Israel four hundred years to repent of her sins while in bondage to the Egyptians. No repentance was shown. When grace was rejected, judgment was inevitable. God's holiness demands justice and righteousness on the part of the sinner. This could only be met in the grace of a loving Christ. He met the just demands of a holy, righteous God. Paul affirms this:

I do not frustrate the grace of God: for if righteousness came by the law, then Christ is dead in vain.

In the parting warning of Moses to Israel, he said:

> When thou comest nigh unto a city to fight against it, then proclaim *peace* unto it. And it shall be, if it make thee answer of peace, and open unto thee, then it shall be, that all the people that is found therein shall be tributaries unto thee, and they shall serve thee. And if it will make no peace with thee, but will make war against thee, then thou shalt besiege it.

Jehovah proclaims grace before judgment. Humanity has always lived in God's "day of grace" from Adam to the present. However, judgment will follow. Grace and mercy have held back its execution.[4]

Some have wondered why Jehovah demanded the utter destruction of the Canaanites. God needs no defense for His actions. His own believe and trust:

> Now we see through a glass, darkly: but then face to face: now I know in part; but then I shall know even as also I am known.

Sodom was the typical city of Canaan. Chastity was unknown, with licentious and unmentionable crimes, worshiping creatures rather than the Creator, and given over to vile passions. However, God in grace extended His mercy to this sinful people. It was either to let the leaven of sin corrupt the whole land, or to exterminate them root and branch for the salvation of future generations. This Jehovah did in grace and mercy. Before destroying Sodom, Jehovah sent Abraham with his godly life to Canaan as an example among them, and later Isaac and Jacob. Even "righteous Lot" for a time showed his displeasure. Melchizedek, the princely priest, lived among them as a benediction for right living, but the Canaanites rejected all the grace and mercy of a loving God.

4. Ruth 1 to 4; Gal. 2:21; Deut. 20:10-12; Eph. 2:5-9

As Noah found grace in the sight of the Lord before the flood, so Hosea described the grace of Christ as the dew of the morning. Salvation by grace was shown to Rahab, the harlot, and her household, included in the covenant of grace made with the spies. Grace begets faith, love, and obedience, not merely human understanding. Solomon said: "Trust in the Lord with all thine heart; and lean not unto thine own understanding." Such grace is offered to sinners today.

Samuel told of grace providing a hiding place in Jehovah whenever sorrow, distress, and persecution arose.

The Psalmist presents the covenant of grace in the protection and security of the believer in the presence of Christ, when he says,

> I will abide in Thy tabernacle for ever; I will trust in the covert of Thy wings.

Twenty-six times we read in Psalm 136: "His mercy endureth forever."

Isaiah tells what the grace of God will do in a dry and barren heart in which He dwells freely:

> The wilderness and the solitary place shall be glad for them; and the desert shall rejoice, and blossom as the rose.

Grace provides a buckler for the believer in Jehovah. "He is a buckler" to all them that trust in Him, for "salvation will God appoint for walls and bulwarks." Because the believer is so helpless, God places his sins upon Christ, hence salvation by grace. "The Lord hath laid on Him the iniquity of us all."

Isaiah gives Jehovah's program of grace:

> The *Spirit* of the *Lord* God is upon *Me* (Trinity shown)
> Anointed [sent] Me to preach good tidings (gospel of grace)

Unto the meek (that repent and believe)
Bind up the broken-hearted (caused by sin)
Proclaim liberty to the captives (in regeneration)
Proclaim the acceptable year of the Lord (year of
   grace).

This the sinner gets through the amazing grace of Jehovah.
However, Isaiah also shows that the day of grace will be
followed by, "The day of vengeance of our God."

The law protects only those who are perfect. Grace has
for its goal perfection, which is Christ-likeness. In grace all
things were created for the glory of God and the good of
humanity. That which is anti-human is anti-God, and what
is anti-God is anti-human. What Moses was not allowed to
do, representing the law based on the covenant of works,
Joshua did, representing grace.

The following contrasts the covenants of law and grace.

LAW	GRACE
Proceeds on the principle that there is good in man to develop.	Recognizes that man is completely ruined and needs a Saviour.
Would merit divine favor.	Extends God's unmerited favor to those under judgment.
Says, "This *do* and live."	Says, "Believe and live— then do."
Says, "Be good and righteous, and I will bless."	Says, "I have blessed, now walk righteously."
Could not bring soul-peace.	Could bring soul-peace.
Leaves the soul in bondage to sin.	Brings liberty.
Sees Israel in Egypt.	Leads to Canaan.
Holds a distance from God.	Draws near to God.
Would leave Moses in Egypt.	Brings Joshua to Canaan.
Deals with self.	Deals with God.
Works from without.	Works from within.
Shuts out from God.	Opens to God.

LAW	GRACE
Points to death.	Points to deliverance.
Is the "letter that killeth."	Makes alive.
Shows what we are.	Shows what God is.
Causes fear.	Brings assurance.
Says, "Do."	Says, "Done."
Brings condemnation.	Brings salvation.
Is grounded in obedience.	Is grounded in Calvary.
Is written on tablets.	Is written on the heart.
Is limited in duration.	Is eternal.
Says, "Earn."	Says, "Take."
Convicts the sinner.	Pardons.
Reforms.	Transforms.
Reveals sin.	Cleanses from sin.
Begins.	Ends.
Blesses the good.	Saves the bad.
Requires righteousness.	Gives righteousness.
Connects with Moses.	Connects with Christ.
Looks to good works.	Looks to saving faith.
Would make man good.	Makes man safe.
Is easily broken by man.	Is everlasting and of God.
Is earthly.	Is heavenly.
Demands the "tithe."	Brings an "offering."
Says, "Wages of sin is death."	Says, "Gift of God—eternal life."
Says, sinner must die.	Says, "I died in Christ."
Demands, "Just with God."	Answers, "Justified in Christ." [5]

5. 1 Cor. 13:12; Psa. 61:4; Proverbs 3:5; Isa. 35:1; 4:6; 32:2; 61:1,2; Rom.
3:21

Chapter 25

CHRIST
*and Security
in the Old Testament*

IN THE STUDY OF NOAH'S ARK WE FIND
an apt type of Christ in salvation and preservation. In this
ship, 300 cubits long, 50 cubits wide, and 30 cubits high, was
ample space for the different species of the land, as well as
for the food. It was made of gopher wood and pitch. Pitch
is seventy times translated, "to make atonement." As the
judgment waters covered all, so death was passed upon all
flesh.

Noah is a type of Christ in that he prepared the ark of
safety, and carried his family above judgment waters. The
ark was God-given for the security of the believers. So are
such secure in Christ.

The Psalmist-shepherd sang in assurance:

Deep calleth unto deep at the noise of thy waterspouts:
all thy waves and thy billows are gone over me.

David knew the security of the mountain fastnesses. They
suggested the Rock of Ages in whom rests eternal security,
hence he sang:

The Lord is my rock, and my fortress, and my deliverer
. . . in whom I will trust; my buckler, and the horn
of my salvation, and my high tower . . . so shall I be
saved. . . .[1]

1. Genesis 6:13,14; 8:4-13; 7:16; Heb. 11:7; Psa. 42:7; 18:2

Dr. Walter Wilson mentions some beautiful individual types of the believer's security in Jehovah. The eagle, a type of Christ in protection and security of His own in sorrow and distress amid the journey of life:

> How I bare you on eagles' wings, and brought you unto myself.
> So that thy youth is renewed like the eagle's.
> They shall mount up with wings as eagles; they shall run, and not be weary; and they shall walk, and not faint.

The ear typifies security in Christ, and the life of obedience to hear and to do His will—a life of service:

> And his master shall bore his ear . . . and he shall serve him forever.

The eye: The Psalmist shows that the eye is a symbol of protection and security. Christ protects His own as the hen covers her own:

> Keep me as the apple of the eye; hide me under the shadow of Thy wings.
> He shall cover thee with His feathers, and under His wings shalt thou trust.

The dove is a type of the sinner who flies to Christ for refuge and security, and confidently trusts His protection:

> Dwell in the rock, and be like the dove that maketh her nest in the sides of the hole's mouth.

The embrace: In the love story of Solomon it typifies security in Christ as a mother would hold her child:

> His left hand is under my head, and his right hand doth embrace me.

The clay is a type of the believer in the hands of the Potter-Christ to be fashioned and molded after the similitude of His likeness:

> Behold, as the clay is in the potter's hand, so are ye in Mine hand.

The feet, recorded by the prophet Habakkuk, tells how Christ will look after and secure His followers in the paths of difficulties:

> The Lord God is my strength and He will make my feet like hinds' feet, and He will make me to walk upon mine high places.

The righteous: Apart from Christ the sinner's righteousness is as "filthy rags" and all unclean. The believer is made the righteousness of God. He imputes to the believer righteousness and charges to His account the sin of the believer.

> And this is His name whereby He shall be called, the Lord our righteousness.

The rock reveals the security of the believer in Christ:

> He only is my rock and my salvation; He is my defence; I shall not be greatly moved.

Here Christ has fenced in His own, protecting those that are upon the Rock.[2]

Every doctrine should be tested as to whether it exalts Christ or man. If it exalts man, it dethrones Christ.

It is not possible for a saved believer to lose his eternal life after having received it as a free gift from God. If man can save himself by his own endeavors, then the glory goes to man and not to God. Salvation is wholly of God. Anything that is *eternal* must be of God.

The Psalmist further sings in his security:

> Though he fall, he shall not be utterly cast down; for the Lord upholdeth him with His hand.

2. Ex. 19:4; Deut. 32:11; Psa. 103:5; Isa. 40:31; Ex. 21:6; Psa. 17:8; Psa. 91:4; Psa. 34:15; 121:3,4; Jer. 48:28; S. of S. 2:6; Jer. 18:6; Isa. 64:8; Hab. 3:19; Jer. 23:6; Rev. 19:8; 3:5; Zech. 3:3,4; Rom. 3:22; Psa. 62:2; Isa. 32:2

I have been young, and now am old; yet have I not seen the righteous forsaken, nor his seed begging bread.

For the Lord loveth judgment, and forsaketh not His saints.

But the salvation of the righteous is of the Lord: He is their strength in time of trouble.

And the Lord shall help them, and deliver them; He shall deliver them from the wicked, and save them, because they trust in Him.

Thou hast thrust sore at me that I might fall: but the Lord helped me.

The Lord is my strength and song, and is become my salvation.

The Lord thinketh upon me: Thou art my help and my deliverer.

The prophet Micah rejoiced in his security, saying:

When I fall, I shall rise; when I sit in darkness, the Lord shall be a light unto me.

King Solomon affirmed this, saying,

A just man falleth seven times, and riseth up again.

Under the Jewish law of the Old Testament, when one was unable to act for himself, the one nearest of kin had a right to act for him. Such was called his *goel*—literally, "kinsman-redeemer." Proverbs records how Christ became *surety* for the debt of sin the unbeliever owes divine justice:

Be not thou one of them that strike hands, or of them that are sureties for debts.

Christ binds Himself as surety for the sin-debt of the seed, His poor kinsmen, whom He represents. Christ took the whole debt upon Himself and became substitute in law. The guilt of the "seed of Abraham" was transferred to Christ, to "restore that which he took not away."

> For He hath made Him to become sin for us, who knew no sin; that we might be made the righteousness of God in Him.

Thus Christ becomes the surety of the believer, giving him "the earnest of the inheritance promised—the sealing of the Holy Spirit." There was an absolute necessity for the Kinsman-Redeemer to become the Surety. The sinner had no standing before God. He was sinful, broken, worthless, with no ability to satisfy the demands of the law. Christ, the Kinsman-Redeemer, became the Surety of the covenant of redemption.

> When we were yet without strength, in due time Christ died for the ungodly.[3]

3. Psa. 37:24,25,28,39,40; 118:13,14; 40:17; Micah 7:8; Prov. 22:26; Rom. 8:1; 2 Cor. 1:12; 5:21; Prov. 24:16

Chapter 26

CHRIST
and Judgment in the Old Testament

GOD MUST BE JUST AS WELL AS MERCIFUL. At the final judgment man's probation forever ceases. God desires that men turn from sin unto Himself. However, because of man's rejection, the Christ-Judge now arises against the wicked to lay judgment to the line, "and righteousness to the plummet."

Whosoever hath sinned against Me, him will I blot out of My book.

Cain confessed his punishment was greater than he could bear. The flood swept the ungodly from the face of the earth. Fire and brimstone were the portion of Sodom and Gomorrah, and Lot's wife met judgment and became a pillar of salt.

Scripture is no less real because it is spoken figuratively or typically. However, prophecy of the future is more difficult of interpretation than that of the past. Many questions are asked about Christ and the judgment to come. "Does death end all?" "Does man enter into another state after death?" "What are the conditions there?" "Is it extinction or immortality?" "Is the future positive or negative?" "What about the love of Christ?"

One should not deny the doctrine of judgment simply because the nature of Christ is love. Both Jesus and John, the "beloved," represent the greatest elements of love, yet they speak most about the judgment awaiting the unbeliever. "It is the voice of divine love heard amid the thunder."

God's problem was to be *just* and to justify the unjust. All the judgment acts of God in the Old Testament were on the basis of justice and righteousness. The sun that vitalized the plant to fruitage destroys the fungus of evil. Acting in accordance with His holiness, God in righteous judgment could have smitten the whole Adamic race and remained just. However, in His infinite love, Christ became a willing Substitute, the righteous claims against the sinner were satisfied, and the believer then is reckoned the righteousness of God in Christ.

Dr. C. I. Scofield says:

> God requires righteousness from man, but saves the unrighteous through sacrifice . . . The Old Testament reveals the justice of God . . . but never in opposition to His mercy.

The glories of a righteous Christ shine forth throughout the Old Testament against the midnight of sin in the world. It was at the midnight of sin that Jehovah delivered Israel from her bondage. Paul and Silas sang praises within the prison walls and were delivered. At midnight of this present age the Deliverer will come and catch His own to Himself.

The Old Testament Scriptures predict the "Day of Jehovah," a day of judgment and wrath to come. As far back as the book of Numbers God had Balaam to prophesy the judgment to come:

> I shall see him, but not now; I shall behold him, but not nigh; there shall come a Star out of Jacob, and a Sceptre shall rise out of Israel, and shall smite the corners of Moab, and destroy all the children of Sheth.

This is a promise of the first coming of the Messiah-Christ as a Star out of Jacob; also, His second coming in judgment as a Sceptre out of Israel. The Star has already shone forth. The Sceptre will yet arise in judgment.

Moses prophesied the Day of Jehovah:

> If I whet my glittering sword, and mine hand take hold on judgment; I will render vengeance to mine enemies, and will reward them that hate me. I will make mine arrows drunk with blood, and my sword shall devour flesh.

Hannah, the old-fashioned mother of Israel, who prayed for a boy-child, ended her prayer and praise to Jehovah in a prophetic judgment:

> The adversaries of the Lord shall be broken to pieces; out of heaven shall He thunder upon them; the Lord shall judge the ends of the earth; and He shall give strength to His King, and exalt the horn of His Anointed.

The first Messianic Psalm warns the nations of the Day of Jehovah in the coming judgment:

> Thou shalt break them with a rod of iron: Thou shalt dash them in pieces like a potter's vessel.

The judgment of the Christ-Judge will not mean total annihilation, but spoiled for its intended use, as implied in the Psalms:

> But those that seek my soul, to destroy it, shall go into the lower parts of the earth.

This represents Christ in judgment, who is able to destroy "both body and soul in hell." [1]

The Judgment Day will be at a time when Christ will judge the unregenerate man. Then the perishing things of

1. Ex. 32:33; 1 Thess. 4:16-18; Num. 24:17; Deut. 32:41,42; 1 Sam. 2:10; Psa. 2:3,9; 37:20; 63:9; Jer. 23:29-32

this life will profit nothing. Solomon, the wise man, gave his experience:

Riches profit not in the day of wrath; but righteousness delivereth from death.

The Psalmist referred to Jehovah-Christ as the Judge of the quick and the dead, who will then reward the saints for their faithfulness, and later judge the wicked that reject His mercy and grace:

For He cometh to judge the earth: He shall judge the world with righteousness, and the people with His truth.

The Psalmist also sang:

Clouds and darkness are round about Him; righteousness and judgment are the habitation of His throne. A fire goeth before Him, and burneth up His enemies round about.

The passage in the Psalms generally used by the advocates for total annihilation is:

But the wicked shall perish, and the enemies of the Lord shall be as the fat of lambs; they shall consume; into smoke shall they consume away.

It will be noticed that this passage has no reference to future retribution, or the immortality of the soul, but to being taken from the earth.

Isaiah records how Jehovah was to preach good tidings and the *vengeance* [judgment] of our God. In Luke's Gospel the Lord omits the word "vengeance," as He was then beginning His dispensation of grace. Judgment was still to follow in the future. Isaiah also prophesied of the Day of the Lord:

For the day of the Lord of hosts shall be upon every one that is proud and lofty, and upon every one that is lifted up; and he shall be brought low . . . Behold, the day of the Lord cometh, cruel both with wrath and fierce anger . . . and He shall destroy the sinners thereof.

Jeremiah prophesied of the judgment in the Day of the Lord:

Ye shall not be unpunished: for I will call for a sword upon all the inhabitants of the earth, saith the Lord of hosts . . . for the Lord hath a controversy with the nations . . . He will give them that are wicked to the sword, saith the Lord . . . Behold, evil shall go forth from nation to nation.[2]

Haggai pictured the Day of the Lord:

I will shake the heavens, and the earth, and the sea, and the dry land; And I will shake all nations . . . And I will overthrow the throne of kingdoms.

The minor prophets often prophesied the judgment:

For the day of the Lord is near upon all the heathen: as thou hast done it shall be done unto thee: thy reward shall return upon thine own head.

The Hebrew meaning of *Joel* is "Jehovah is God." This prophet refers five times to the Day of Judgment.

The sun and the moon shall be darkened, and the stars shall withdraw their shining. The Lord also shall roar out of Zion and utter His voice from Jeruselem; and the heavens and the earth shall shake.

Amos began his prophecy with judgment:

And he said, the Lord will roar from Zion, and utter His voice from Jerusalem; and the habitations of the shepherds shall mourn, and the top of Carmel shall wither.

Micah described the Day of Jehovah:

2. Prov. 11:4; Psa. 96:13; 97:2,3; 37:20; Isa. 61:2; 2:12-21; 13:6,9; Mal. 4:5; Jer. 25:29-32; 30:23,24; Matt. 12:18-20

And I will execute vengeance in anger and fury upon the heathen, such as they have not heard.

The meaning of the word *Zephaniah* is "Jehovah hides." His prophecy of the Day of Jehovah tells of a dreadful future that awaits the impenitent:

The great day of the Lord is near, it is near, and hasteth greatly, even the voice of the day of the Lord; the mighty man shall cry there bitterly. That day is a day of wrath, a day of trouble and distress, a day of wasteness and desolation, a day of darkness and gloominess, a day of clouds and thick darkness.

Malachi ("My messenger"), the last of the prophets, gave a graphic picture of the Day of Jehovah:

For, behold, the day cometh, that shall burn as an oven; and all the proud, yea, and all that do wickedly, shall be stubble: and the day that cometh shall burn them up, saith the Lord of hosts, that it shall leave them neither root nor branch.

Malachi designates Jehovah as the "Sun of Righteousness" with healing in His wings, but a people can become so corrupt as to compel God to destroy them. The moral nature of God revolts against unrighteousness as light against darkness, health against disease, purity against impurity, holiness against unholiness. What the sun is to the universe, Christ is to the spiritual man. The sun softens wax, but hardens clay; dispels darkness with light, and cold with heat. It is the nature of water to soften, but it also petrifies. "I loved Jacob and I hated Esau." Malachi brings the message of the love of Jehovah, but is burdened with the sins of the priests and the people. His prophecy ends with the Day of the Lord in judgment. He sees both Advents of the Lord blended in one, with two aspects—love and law. The first foretells the forerunner, and afterward the coming of the Messenger of the Covenant in His Second Advent. Malachi enumerates the deadly sins and failure of Israel: profaning and polluting the table of the Lord; the priests causing many to stumble; dealing "treacherously against his brother"; "Judah . . . hath married the daughter of a strange god"; saying, "Every one that doeth evil is good"; robbing God "in tithes and offerings."

All this sinning was in spite of a loving Jehovah. Israel's moral judgment was perverted; giving bitter for sweet, evil for good, darkness for light. "Motive determines action. Destiny hangs on choice." Luxury and evil were Israel's motivating power. Trying to keep all, Israel lost all. God demands spiritual fruitage.[3]

Dr. Walter Wilson in his book on "Types" calls attention to the following: The fan, a type of Christ in wrath and judgment upon those who reject His mercy and grace:

I will fan them . . . I will bereave them . . . I will destroy . . . since they return not from their ways.

The fingers of judgment continually point to the doomed that reject the overtures of Jehovah:

In the same hour came forth fingers of a man's hand, and wrote over against the candlestick.

The cup, typifying the judgments of Jehovah, when the sinner will be forced to drink it:

Awake, awake, stand up, O Jerusalem, which hast drunk at the hand of the Lord the cup of His fury; thou hast drunken the dregs of the cup of trembling, and wrung them out.

Thou art filled with shame for glory . . . the cup of the Lord's right hand shall be turned unto thee, and shameful spewing shall be on thy glory.

3. Haggai 2:6,7,22; Obadiah 15; Joel 2:10; Amos 1:2; Micah 5:15; Zeph. 1:14,15; Mal. 1:4; 4:1; Isa. 41:16; Hab. 2:16; Isa. 51:17

The ax is a type of one whom Jehovah uses to punish another:

Assyria was the ax in the hands of the Lord.

Shall the ax boast itself against Him that heweth therewith?

The balances are types of judgment to satisfy the just demands of the law, and when the sinner tears asunder the "Bands" of restraint:

Let us break their bands asunder, and cast away their cords from us.

Thou art weighed in the balances, and art found wanting.

Brimstone is a telling type of the destructive wrath of Jehovah poured out in judgment:

The pile thereof is fire and much wood; the breath of the Lord, like a stream of brimstone, doth kindle it.

The chambers typify the apartments in hell where sinners are punished:

Her house is the way to hell, going down to the chambers of death.[4]

After His hungry disciples had plucked the ears of corn, seeing the Pharisees taking counsel against Him, Christ uttered those memorable words of the prophet Isaiah:

Behold My servant, whom I have chosen; My beloved in whom My soul is well pleased; I will put My Spirit upon Him, and He shall show judgment to the Gentiles.

The Bible prophesies three distinct judgments for the believer: first, the judgment of the believer's sins on the

4. Jer. 15:7; Matt. 3:12; Dan. 5:5; Isa. 51:17; Jer. 25:15-17,28; Dan. 5:27; Isa. 10:15; Psa. 2:3; Isa. 30:33; Prov. 7:27

Cross, Christ being judged in lieu of the sinner; secondly, the judgment of the believer's self, for self-crucifixion and self-abnegation; thirdly, the judgment of the believer's works at the bema (judgment seat) of Christ. This at His Second Advent to reward His own for faithfulness.

Finally, there will be a judgment of the unsaved. This will take place before God, the Judge, at the Great White Throne Judgment, resulting in eternal damnation. Christ in judgment will finally destroy His enemies, the beast, antichrist, the devil, with all his followers:

> Their wine is the poison of dragons, and the cruel venom of asps . . . I will make My arrows drunk with blood, and My sword shall devour flesh.

> And He laid hold on the dragon, that old serpent, which is the Devil, and Satan, and bound him a thousand years, and cast him into the bottomless pit, . . . that he should deceive the nations no more.

The Old, as well as the New Testament declares that God is a "consuming fire." [5]

5. Isa. 42:1-3; Matt. 12:18; Deut. 32:33,42; Rev. 20:2,3,15; Deut. 32:42

Chapter 27

CHRIST
in Genesis and Revelation

GENESIS IS A GREEK WORD MEANING "generation" or "beginning." The Hebrew word is *bereshith* meaning "in the beginning." Many consider Genesis the most important book in the Bible. It is not speculation, but revelation; not fiction, but fact. Genesis affirms the divine origin of the universe and the human race. It tells of creation, the home, the Sabbath, temptation, the fall of man, and redemption provided by the shedding of blood.

Genesis presents Satan, the tempter, with man's privilege of choice and his yielding to sin. It is the foundation of man's first knowledge of God. Nature speaks, but fails to give the moral attributes of God, or the remedy for sin. What nature cannot teach is revealed in this first book of the Bible. This book reveals God and His will. God is greater than His Word only in the sense that the One revealed is greater than the instrument which reveals Him.

In Genesis, Christianity finds its inspiration; in Revelation, its final expression. In Genesis is foundation; in Revelation is consummation. Genesis reveals the beginning of all things; Revelation makes known the end.

Revelation, in the main, points back to the Old Testament. The comparison of Genesis with the Revelation presents God's eternal purpose in history as a spiritual one. A study of this comparison will strengthen the faith of the Bible student, enrich his life and anchor him firmly in that "blessed hope."

Revelation (Greek, *apocalypse*) means unveiling, or un-covering; setting forth the divine program of God in Christ. Many have been the schemes of interpretation sought for this book. That which makes it historical to the close of chapter three, and future from chapter six seems most satisfactory.

The Revelation shows the end of earthly empires and the rule of man, just as Genesis shows the beginning. Urquhart wrote:

> If we produce a Book in which predictions, so numer-ous and varied and minute as to preclude all possibility of change, were recorded centuries before the events occurred in which they were startlingly fulfilled, will it be any longer possible to doubt that God is, and that this Book is His word to us?

Genesis and Revelation give certain strong links that unite the beginning and the ending of the Scriptures. These dem-onstrate the unity of authorship and design of the Scriptures. With hundreds of years intervening between the writings, there appears perfect unity and accord. It must have been the unity of the Scriptures as here given that would cause the French rationalist, Jean Jacques Rousseau, to say: "I must confess to you that the majesty of the Scriptures as-tonishes me."

Attention has been called to the following links between these two books.

GENESIS [1]	REVELATION [2]
"In the beginning God."	"I Am . . . the beginning," Christ.
"The heaven and the earth."	The new heaven and earth.
"Darkness upon . . . the deep."	"No night there"—Christ is the Light.
"Let there be light."	"The Lamb is the light thereof."

1. Gen. 1:1,2,3,10,16; 2:4,9,11,12, 15-22; 4:17; 3:1,4,7,8,15-19,24

2. Rev. 22:13; 21:1; 22:5; 21:23; 21:1,5; 22:2,16; 21:18,19; 21:2,3; 21: 27; 19:8; 21:3,4,24; 22:3,14; 21; 22

GENESIS	REVELATION
Water called the seas.	Christ, the water of life.
"The stars also."	I AM "the bright and morning Star."
"They were created."	"Behold, I make all things new," re-created.
"The tree of life."	Christ is "The tree of life."
"In the midst of the garden."	"In the midst of the street of it [the New Jerusalem]."
"Land . . . where there is gold."	"The streets of heaven are of gold."
Land of precious stones.	Christ is "that Rock," precious stone.
City built by Cain.	"City whose builder and maker is God."
City *going up* on earth.	City *coming down* from God.
God communed with man.	Christ will dwell with men.
A bride presented to Adam.	"A bride adorned for her husband."
The serpent deceiving.	The serpent cast into the lake of fire.
First lie entered the earth.	Nothing "that maketh a lie."
Man clothed with fig leaves.	Man clothed in "fine linen" (Christ's righteousness).
First man Adam caused mankind to be lost.	Last man Adam caused nations to be saved.
Man hiding from the face of God.	Christ face-to-face with man.
Pain and sorrow were decreed.	Christ conquers pain and sorrow.
Death decreed because of Adam's sin.	"No more death" because Christ conquered it.
Curse pronounced.	"No more curse," in Christ.
God's commandments broken.	"They do His commandments."
Adam shut out from the Tree of Life.	Christ proved right to the "Tree of Life."
The great promise of the "Seed" is given.	The great promise of the "Seed" is fulfilled in Christ.

INDEX TO NAMES OF JEHOVAH